The Lie We Like Best

The Lie We Like Best

How We Exchanged the Truth of God for a Man-Made Lie

Graeme Schultz

Gobsmacked Publishing

Copyright © 2016 Graeme Schultz

TAll Scripture quotations, unless otherwise indicated, are taken from the Holy Bible, New International Version®, NIV®. Copyright ©1973, 1978, 1984, 2011 by Biblica, Inc.™ Used by permission of Zondervan. All rights reserved worldwide. www.zondervan.com The "NIV" and "New International Version" are trademarks registered in the United States Patent and Trademark Office by Biblica, Inc.™

All rights reserved. No part of this publication may be reproduced, distributed or transmitted in any form or by any means, including photocopying, recording, or other electronic or mechanical methods, without the prior written permission of the publisher, except in the case of brief quotations embodied in critical reviews and certain other noncommercial uses permitted by copyright law. For permission requests, write to the publisher, addressed "Permissions Coordinator," at the address below.

Graeme Schultz/Gobsmacked Publishing

19 Trotters Lane, Cudgee, Victoria, Australia, 3265.

www.gobsmackedpublishing.com.au

National Library of Australia Cataloguing-in-Publication Entry

Creator: Schultz, Graeme, author.

Title: Back in the garden again : the mystery hidden for ages, and now revealed to us / Graeme Schultz.

ISBN: 9780994603029 (paperback)

ISBN: 9780994603036 (ebook)

Subjects: Christian life.

Spiritual life–Christianity.

God–Knowableness.

God–Love.

Dewey Number: 248.4

Dedicated to all who have found the 'one thing'…
- Christ and Him crucified -

Contents

AUTHOR'S NOTE:	1
INTRODUCTION.	3
Chapter 1. Lies Are Everywhere.	5
Chapter 2. The Premise Problem.	11
Chapter 3. The First Lie.	19
Chapter 4. Whose Idea Was The Law?	25
Chapter 5. Why Did Christ Come?	29
Chapter 6. Religion V. Faith.	35
Chapter 7. The Battle For Our Minds.	39
Chapter 8. We Must Die Before We Can Live.	45
Chapter 9. Putting 'No Confidence' In The Flesh.	51
Chapter 10. The Heart Transplant We Had To Have.	55
Chapter 11. Letting Go.	61
Chapter 12. Life On The Other Side.	65
Chapter 13. How Big Is Our Salvation?	71
Chapter 14. Seated In Heavenly Places.	75
Chapter 15. Disposing Of The Lie.	79
Chapter 16. Indestructible Life.	85
Chapter 17. The Father's Heart.	91

Chapter 18. Life-Principles V. Surrender.   99
Chapter 19. The Spirit Gives Life.   105
Chapter 20. The Foot Of The Cross.   111
Chapter 21. He Lives My Life.   117
CONCLUSION.   121

AUTHOR'S NOTE:

My intention in writing this book has been to show that there is a lie that has been written on the hearts of humanity ever since Adam took leave of the presence of God. This lie obscures the very thing we want most – the Life of the Spirit.

The way to this life is a narrow, less crowded road - and few find it. Yet it awaits us all.

I have deliberately written in a way that is more conversational than instructional. My intention in this conversation is not to tell you how to think or believe; only you can do that. Rather, I have described a foundational premise that underpins our thinking and influences every aspect of our Christianity. It is the same premise that has caused Adam (and all his offspring since), to misunderstand the heart of God.

We exchanged the truth of God for a man-made lie and we don't even know it… but Jesus came to remove the lie - and give us himself in its place.

INTRODUCTION.

Have you ever attempted a Sudoku puzzle *(you know the ones; number puzzles - 9 high x 9 wide)?* I occasionally try to solve one, and even enjoyed a reasonable success rate - I'm no genius, but I have managed to complete quite a few over the years.

Sudoku puzzles come in several categories – *easy, hard, and very hard.* I usually go straight for the tough ones; I like to apply myself to the thing, so I generally choose a puzzle that will challenge me. It's a matter of working at it until some of the numbers drop into place – once you have a few solved, the rest of the puzzle generally follows.

Occasionally I get stuck. I try every angle I can think of – but the breakthrough doesn't come.

I know the puzzle can be solved because the answers are found over the page, but it's like a log-jam of numbers that won't give up – it seems 'so close, yet so far'. I know that if I can get just one thing to click in to place then the rest of the puzzle will probably follow, so I look at the puzzle from every angle – *but I can't find the one thing.*

There are some people who have a head for solving Sudoku's; they never seem to get stuck. They are able to look at the puzzle in a different way to me, and see things I don't see. It's like they have a sixth sense for working out Sudoku's, an ability that goes beyond the norm; *they can look with different eyes, and see the 'one thing' that I can't.*

They may not be a genius; they just seem to see things I can't. They seem to be wired up to view the thing on a different plane... *and the numbers just fall into place.*

For me, Christianity and Sudoku puzzles have some things in common.

Over the years I have managed the Christian puzzle quite well – I can usually find the answers to life's mysteries, or at least work my way through until the answers appear.

Occasionally life has dealt me a puzzle I couldn't solve, *(and to make matters worse my Christian belief system didn't seem to hold the answers either).* I know deep down that hidden somewhere within Christianity all the issues of life are answered, but the missing link is elusive – *like the Sudoku, the solution lays beyond my grasp.*

At this point I wonder if it is just me. I wonder if some people can view their Christianity differently to me, and see things I don't see. It would be like a sixth sense – an ability that sees beyond the obvious. Not that they would necessarily be more spiritual or religious than me, but - *when they look at the same information I do, they see an entirely different view.*

It is this different view that holds the key.

I used to get stuck because I couldn't see beyond the immediate and the obvious, and view into the deeper information of my faith – it was like I had a road-block wired into my brain that held me back.

I am relieved to say that the ability to 'see the missing thing' that I have described above, has now become my normal experience... *I have found 'the one thing'.*

To become this person I had to erase a lie from my mind. It was a lie that lived in the very core of my being – and it obstructed from view the truth that was before me the whole time.

Chapter 1.
Lies Are Everywhere.

Some lies are relatively benign; they carry no great capacity to do harm. 'Do these pants make me look fat?' (...*to lie, or not to lie*).

Sometimes a little stretching of the truth seems like the kindest response to make. Sure; it may lead the person who is concerned about their appearance to embark on a course more ambitious than they should… but in the bigger scheme of things, there are times when it's better to ere on the side of generosity - than absolute truth.

The fact is; there are times when we don't want the truth – we would rather opt for a believable lie.

It's not so much that we are bent on deception; it's more about having a convenient view of the facts, a view that interprets reality in a way that agrees with us - *for whatever reason*. Dishonesty is not our intention, but rather a presentation of the facts that embraces the greater good… *as we see it*.

Stay with me now… this is heading somewhere!

Absolute truth can be inconvenient; it can often run counter to the direction we have already determined to take / or the world we have constructed for ourselves. We would prefer a measured version of the truth, one that contains part of the absolute truth, as well as an acknowledgment of the world as we think it ought to be.

Just like the person who asks "do these pants make me look fat", we want a response that agrees with the course we have already chosen - we want truth to agree with us, not the other way around.

It seems that we are wired-up that way;
We come with a built-in disposition,
it causes us to perceive reality as we think it should be,
and then manipulate the facts to suit.

We are by nature able to adjust the workings of our mind in such a way that this 'built-in disposition' is elevated above absolute truth. It's not intended as deliberate deception, but merely a creative use of the facts to support our pre-determined position.

I am raising all of this to highlight a very serious problem that besets Christians. Human beings are not by nature wired-up to do truth particularly well, we have a lie written into our hearts that changes everything – *we just don't realize that it is there.* The human race inherited a lie from Adam that has become so deeply built-in to our nature, and we are so completely 'at home' with it, that we don't question its validity.

When Adam chose independence from God, his ability to grasp truth was one of the major casualties. He gave up his built-in truth compass, and exchanged it for a self-based lie… from that moment on; everything would pass through the filter of his self-oriented reality.

For truth to be truth, it would have to pass the self-test.

It is this fact that satan has exploited.

Satan was stripped of his power at the cross; he has no ability to do us harm. Christ has made a public spectacle of satan's downfall, and all he has left now is the power of deceptive suggestion. Christ came to destroy the works of the enemy – *and we know he was successful;* so it follows that satan has been stripped of his ability to wreck havoc upon us… now he is merely left with lies.

He is the master liar.

The question for Christians is this; "What lie is satan likely to promote to do us the most harm?"

Some will say; 'that's easy – he will tempt us to sin'… others will add; 'he will try to stop us doing good and being active in the Christian life'… *the possibilities are endless.*

I believe satan has just one lie that he repeats over and over, a lie that he has used to bring down the union that Adam and Eve first enjoyed with God - and it is a lie that has been written on human hearts ever since. This one lie is presented in a variety of ways depending on the person and circumstance involved, but it is based on the one destructive notion that has been bringing mankind unstuck throughout all of history.

It is a lie that is so believable, that we the human race, are drawn to it like a moth to a flame – it is indeed 'The lie we like best'.

> *The lie is not complicated,*
> *nor is it particularly focused on causing us to sin;*
> *it is a simple, short, 3 word lie –*
> *"The flesh counts".*

There; it doesn't sound so scary does it? Certainly not scary enough to be the mother of all satanic lies… *but it is!* The lie 'that the flesh counts' is built so deeply into us that we would never consider examining its validity… *(Some things simply don't need to be examined).*

That's the truly sinister part; it seems so benign, *like a harmless throw-away line.* It just doesn't seem to have the capacity to bring the human race unstuck.

Jesus said in John 6:63 'The Spirit gives life, <u>the flesh counts for nothing</u>'.

It's not immediately obvious why this is so important. We acknowledge that it may indeed be true, but it just doesn't seem terribly important in the bigger scheme of things. It's one of those statements that we read-over and put to one side - *as a part of the general conversation that Jesus had as he moved about in Galilee.*

Never-the-less it is a motherhood statement that clarifies the human condition like no other, it goes to the very heart of the problem of people in all ages, cultures and pursuits.

The importance of Jesus words cannot be grasped without a clear understanding of the problem with humanity. We need to go all the way back to Eden and look again at what went wrong, then understand afresh why Jesus came and exactly what he accomplished in coming. And finally we need to grasp anew what this means for us now.

At first glance John 6:63 appears to be a fairly general admonition from Jesus that we should avoid the excesses of indulgent living - that he is exhorting us to live a stoic life of self-control that keeps a wide berth of the passions of the flesh.

But the problem for us is that we have read this scripture through the very lens that it is condemning – *(without realizing it)*. The lie that is written on our hearts distorts the truth, with the result that we arrive at a conclusion which is at polar opposites of its real meaning.

The flesh is like that.
It distorts truth to shape reality to suit itself.

So it stands to reason that the flesh will miss-interpret these words of Jesus, *which so directly put the flesh in its proper place.* <u>The flesh wants to count</u> - *but* <u>*the Spirit cannot give life while it does.*</u>

The flesh doesn't count – at least, not in the way we might think it does. Sure the actions of the flesh contribute to our identity on planet earth, but these actions contribute nothing to our standing with God – *for that only the blood of Christ counts.*

But first we must go back to the start, and gain a fresh understanding of the flesh, the Spirit, and the problem that we (the human race) inherited from Adam.

Chapter 2.
The Premise Problem.

BEHIND everything we believe, lays a premise.

This premise is the foundational belief upon which our more conscious thoughts are layered.

The Oxford dictionary describes a 'premise' as a previous statement from which another is inferred. Everything we believe is supported by a deeper foundational position we hold to be true. We may be convinced that our belief system is pure, and independent of other influences or opinions - but in reality, what we believe is more likely a conscious thought / we have applied over something hidden much deeper down. *Something that seems so right that we would never question it.*

Beneath everything we believe are convictions that we do not give much consideration to. It is these subconsciously held values that are the field where satan has sown his lie. They are convictions that we consider non-negotiable facts, and so their authenticity is never properly scrutinized or tested.

Even though we think our lives are under the direction of our day-to-day reasoning and decision making, in reality they are directed by foundational convictions that are buried far more deeply inside. These foundational beliefs direct our lives at a subconscious level – we are so *'at home'* with them that they have become the undisputed truth of our lives.

As an example of this, let's say that the premise we hold is that the world is flat *(there was a time when that was an undisputed truth, based on the observations of the majority)*. If you were a maritime navigator this premise could seriously limit your travels. You may have had all the available maps and charts, you may have understood the stars, the currents and the tides – but if your underlying premise was wrong then everything else has been built upon miss-information. Your ability to perform in the vocation you have chosen would be drastically hampered by this one foundational error – *(even though everything else you know may be correct)*. Your knowledge of matters pertaining to navigation on the high seas may be unsurpassed – but the fact remains; **a vast amount of correct information laid over an incorrect premise, does not cause the premise to become correct.**

Imagine now that the premise you hold is that 'the flesh counts' - this premise is the undisputed truth that is widely accepted. It has at its heart the notion that 'how we conduct ourselves' is the primary ingredient required to construct a meaningful life on planet earth. Our words and actions validate us before God, and also with the people we are contact, as we live our lives.

But what if the notion that 'the flesh counts', is even more outdated than 'the world is flat'.

Though it is based on the practical observations of the majority, it remains a hang-over from a by-gone era – it is a premise that has been superseded by the work of Christ. Yet, this premise remains in operation because the alternative 'The Spirit gives life' seems as unlikely as 'the world is round'. All of the evidence supports the notion that 'the flesh counts' - *except the voice of the Spirit of God.*

Everyone has a life based on premises or convictions. We may not consciously know they are there, we may not know where they came from, and we may not be able to articulate them in real terms, but they are there anyway – deeply directing our journey through life. They are built into us by our upbringing, experiences, <u>and most importantly - by our fallen nature</u>.

Chapter 2. The Premise Problem.

In the Christian context these premises are of vital importance; *life and death importance.*

Every human being is born with the premise that 'the flesh counts', it is wired into us as Adam's descendants. When we became believers Christ gave us a new nature, and it is now up to us to live in that new nature. This new nature is every bit our real identity, the old nature is gone – our part is to bring our thinking into agreement with our new nature.

> *To do that we must erase the lie that we inherited from Adam, and re-build upon the truth.*

'The flesh counts' is the defining premise that has underpinned the thinking of humanity since Adam took leave of God's presence. This premise has caused us to miss-understand the role of our personal behavior and lifestyle as the 'means' by which we please or move God – *the pleasure of God is ours simply because we are hidden in Christ.* In that regard; 'the flesh counts for nothing' - it is only as we put aside the *security* we construct from our good deeds and lifestyle, and cling to Christ alone, that the pleasure of God can truly rest upon us.

It is not that we abandon a lifestyle of respectability and honesty - but that we cease to live that way as our means of shoring-up our security with God. Our security is placed entirely upon the shoulders of Jesus – *our 'right living' is simply the overflow.*

This 'lifestyle-focused' form of Christianity has placed a vast amount of information onto the minds of the great congregation of believers – information that is more about us and how we live, than about Jesus. We are like sponges for this new religious information. We soak it in, and attempt to construct the best life possible from it. We are drawn to the language and lifestyle of the masses, and there is never a shortage of new and compelling stuff to choose from.

Our problem is not that we want for spiritual information; it is that we overlay this information onto an incorrect foundation. As I said earlier: *a vast amount of correct information laid over an incorrect premise, does not cause the premise to become correct.*

'The Spirit gives Life' and 'the flesh counts' are opposing premises – they do not exist in tandem, or work together co-operatively.

In this regard satan does not have to tell us a vast number of lies. He does not need to undermine a myriad of spiritual truths, or feed us a diverse array of misleading and deceitful thoughts – all he needs to do is lay a false foundation.

He has mastered his work; he knows exactly what to say so that we will swallow without question the un-godliest premise ever told - "The Flesh Counts".

That is not to say that our human existence is invalid or irrelevant, or that a life full of good deeds and service is un-necessary, but rather that God never intended for it to be the source from which we draw our identity. He had something far higher in mind - *that we would find our very identity and sense of worth in our union with him.*

> *Even the most noble of Christian service and pursuits,*
> *and the most penetrating and impressive theology is irrelevant,*
> *if it becomes our focus – rather than Christ himself.*

Perhaps one of the most alarming aspects of Christianity today is that we amass such a vast diversity of Christian information. We are like travellers on the great Christian information highway - collecting a wide range of spiritual souvenirs along the way, and adding them to our extensive library of useful spiritual facts.

Philippians 3:8 stands in stark contrast; Paul goes to great lengths to articulate the foundation upon which his life is built; he considers everything a loss compared to the surpassing greatness of knowing Christ Jesus. Similarly in

Chapter 2. The Premise Problem.

1 Corinthians 2:2 he says "For I resolved to know nothing while I was with you except Jesus Christ and him crucified".

Paul was different to the modern Christian; he didn't care for a vast accumulation of spiritual information, only one thing mattered - 'Christ'. Paul lived his life from this one foundational premise, and everything else was relegated to the category of mere rubbish - of no more importance than background noise. Paul lived the most energetic life of service imaginable – yet it was Christ himself *(not his own life of service)* that filled his thoughts.

Again, in 1 Corinthians 3:11, "For no one can lay any foundation other than the one already laid, which is Jesus Christ." The premise upon which Paul founded his life was Christ alone; his spiritual library contained just one volume – Christ.

Paul chose to know just one thing.

The reason many Christians today remain on an ongoing quest to find God, is that they don't know the one thing that Paul did. They are in an endless pursuit of trying to make sense of the 'flesh's need to count' - it's a lifelong pilgrimage to God, giving him their best in the hope of somehow touching his divine presence. But it's a life constructed on a wrong foundation, they don't need to seek God - *he has already made his home in us.*

All the spiritual information in the world, and all of the church's activities and pursuits (no matter how impressive and altruistic they seem) - do not come close to the wonder of knowing Christ alone.

The modern church has presented us with such a vast and diverse array of Christian information and activities, that we hardly know how to find Christ. We make the mistake of thinking that he is inside the myriad stuff of Christianity, but he is not found there – to find him we must take a personal journey to the cross.

Like the navigator of old; we may have everything right - except for the premise upon which this right information in laid. If we set sail on our life's journey with the wrong basic premise, then the wind that fills our sails may be mere human effort instead of the breath of God, and our journey of faith will be seriously limited.

The only foundation that counts is Christ – all other information and activity *(no matter how spiritual it sounds)* must be considered inferior to the mysterious truth which is found in him.

This is more than awarding him 'naming rights' for the movement we have developed in his honor, it is more than giving him a respectful nod, then getting on with the busy life we call Christianity – it is more akin to filling our whole screen with Christ as the filter through which every ambition and pursuit must pass.

By-and-large; we don't know how to give Christ the whole screen of our lives.

In Hebrews 12:2 we read, "Let us fix our eyes on Jesus the author and perfecter of our faith". We cannot fix our eyes on two objects *(we would go cross-eyed)* – we either fix them on Jesus / or on ourselves. We are either focused on making the flesh count by a 'good-living' form of Christianity / or we are focused on Christ, and allowing the 'Life of his Spirit' to fill us.

The realm of nature in which we live (this physical existence); was never intended by God as the vehicle we would use to construct a meaningful life. We were designed to find true meaning elsewhere, in our true home - *God himself*. Nature was only ever given as a gift to be enjoyed, to reign over, to experience as an expression of God's love – but never as the arena in which we would find our identity. Our 'good living' must only ever be the natural overflow of reveling in the goodness of Christ.

'The flesh counts' - is the realm of nature, competing with God for our identity.

Chapter 2. The Premise Problem.

In the chapters that follow I would like to explore the importance of building our faith upon one premise, one foundational truth. I would like to consider the difference between the two foundational positions "the flesh counts" and "the flesh counts for nothing" and compare the outcomes they produce.

From way back in the Garden of Eden - to Christianity in this present day, these premises have sent well-meaning Christians in polar opposite directions. There are a few that have ventured on a road less crowded, and the far-off look in their eye reveals an authenticity most never experience – *these are the ones who have discovered the 'one thing'.*

If you want all of the trappings of the great big culture called Christianity then this book may not resonate with your heart, if on the other hand you have had your fill of the hype and want what Paul had – then the 'one thing' you desire may be closer than you think.

Chapter 3.
The First Lie.

Adam had it made. God gave him the whole ball game. Not only did he create Adam in his own image, but he gave him dominion over everything living thing on the planet – everything that had life in it was God's gift to him.

Adam didn't have to check with God for anything. God simply tossed him the keys to his great creation and said; "here, take it for a spin, it's yours now… enjoy!"

But that wasn't all, God gave him a perfect heart – he gave him his own nature. He did this so they could enjoy unbroken fellowship together – Adam and God had the most intimate and connected union possible. Holiness is like that; fellowship is just there - *between people who share the same image*. Adam didn't need to do fellowship with God, or deliberately engage with him, they were in perfect union continuously – Adam knew it and he reveled in it.

What a life; Adam was *(in-effect)* the god of all the material world, and he had unbroken fellowship with the most High God of All. And God even added more – he gave him a perfect woman to share it all with.

Imagine a typical day for Adam and Eve; they were free to rule and reign over all creation, they had deep fellowship with their amazing God / Father who started the whole thing, and they enjoyed a perfect love for each other

– sharing experiences beyond any man or woman since… *because everything was still un-spoiled.*

They had no consciousness of right or wrong; such thinking was foreign to them because their deeds did not establish their worth or identity; this was a free gift from God himself. They never contemplated the notion of doing something because it was the 'right thing' to do; they just lived abundantly because it was their nature to do so. They naturally drew on their union with God as their source of life - *so everything they did produced life.*

This is hard for us to grasp; we don't readily understand the notion of living without a consciousness of right and wrong. We imagine that without the exercising of good decision making we will slip-up in some way – it is hard for us to imagine how we might live a good life, without consciously choosing to do so.

It is one of the most remarkable contrasts between the way people live today, and the way Adam and Eve lived in the beginning. They never once chose to do good, there was no choice to make, they were simply good through-and-through by nature *(God's nature)*, – they lived in innocent disregard for evil because they didn't know what it was.

This kind of living gave then a great sense of security; they understood that holiness and righteousness filled their spirit - simply because they were in beautiful union with the one who was truly holy and righteous. It didn't come down to how well they lived, but rather whether they reveled and rested in the flow of life *(that divine vitality)*, that passed continuously from God into them.

They contemplated no other way to live because there was no other way – *God gave life,* it was how it all worked. Not that God expected anything in return, or patronized Adam and Eve with his charitable ways; quite the contrary – God simply <u>gave</u> life because he <u>was</u> life. This life flowed spontaneously from his being, and Adam and Eve bathed in it and fed on it because it was so wonderful to be the objects of God's love.

Chapter 3. The First Lie.

What could satan do against such bliss? What possible lie could he put forward that could unsettle such a perfect union?

He couldn't suggest that God didn't love them because he clearly did. He couldn't tell them that God was unhappy with how they were living, because they had no idea what good or bad living was. He couldn't promise them success, wealth or beauty because they already had all those things – they were complete in every way possible.

So he decided to perpetrate a lie that had the appearance of enhancing their existence rather than harming it; he put forward a notion so simple and so subtle that it sounded like music to their ears – satan offered them the knowledge of good and evil; he offered them a new way to view life. This new information contained within it the notion that they could be like God, and generate their own righteousness through their own right living.

They could do all this from within themselves; 'because the flesh counts'.

All he had to do was turn their gaze toward themselves and away from God, and he had them. It all came down to who they 'fixed their eyes on' for their spiritual sustenance.

The truly sinister part is that Adam and Eve probably had no intention of doing evil; they just wanted to try out being their own independent source of life. They were not focused on any bad thing; they just wanted a crack at producing their own self-generated choices and outcomes.

> *This new information unveiled good and evil to them.*
> *Now the life that flowed through them would be the result*
> *of their own actions,*
> *their juggling of good and evil would become the channel for a happy life.*

It was that simple; all satan had to do was suggest that they could produce their own life-giving righteousness – what could be more reasonable than that. *"God does it... so we can too!"*

The lie was not so much aimed at getting them to do evil; it was to convince them that they had it within themselves to produce life. The part that satan didn't explain was that God couldn't share the life-giving role; it wouldn't be possible for Adam and Eve to do their bit / and for God to do his bit. It had to be all or nothing – *and Adam and Eve inadvertently chose nothing.*

The result was that God allowed them the independence they wanted, but at such a price – Adam and Eve began a life that took sole responsibility for itself. In the place of holy naked innocence, they had to clothe themselves with their own goodness… *day-in day-out.*

The lie had taken hold.

The fact is; satan didn't need to tempt them to sin, he just needed to convince them to leave home - *to leave the Tree of Life.* Once he had them dining on the wrong tree, sin would be crouching at the door, ready to master anyone who was in the self-righteousness game - Genesis 4:7.

Perhaps the greatest casualty of all was the change to their nature. One day they were filled with the very heart of God; *his holiness, his character, and his life* - the next day they were devoid of God, depending on their own goodness to carve out a meaningful life.

> ***God had to step away,***
> ***they would never manage to attain from within themselves***
> ***the virtue required to share his presence.***

For the first time in history the saddest of all laments rang out – "My God, my God, why have you forsaken me?"

Much later, these same words became the morbid lament of Jesus as the failed experiment of Adam came surging into his pure heart. That terrible moment in time when he took the fallen nature of humanity into himself on the cross, is the very same echo of all humanity - since Adam and Eve struck out on their own.

Chapter 3. The First Lie.

*The righteous God cannot co-habituate
with the self-righteous man.*

This man that was made in God's image… but chose instead to generate a new image from his own flesh. This man that embarked on the most foolish experiment in human history… to prove that the flesh counts.

What then is the flesh? It is the nature of man / without the life giving righteousness of God to keep it.

It is the human heart that has left its home in God, and set up residence in itself.

It is not so much that it is bad, but rather that it has chosen independence from God's goodness – it is a self-based nature, a nature that tries to be good and can't because it wasn't designed to produce goodness… *it was designed to carry it within.*

Don't be fooled; the flesh is not merely rampant self-indulgent behavior – it is independence from God.

Did satan tempt Adam and Eve to sin? Not directly – he simply convinced them that they could be god for themselves. He convinced them that a nature that was not sustained by God's righteousness could turn to itself for righteousness – and the flesh nature was born, the lie was inscribed on their hearts.

*And so began the most ambitious endeavor in all human history
to make the flesh count.*

I am reluctant to leave the subject of 'the flesh' yet as a misunderstanding of it's true meaning will leave us back where we started – believing a lie.

The flesh is not merely the motivator of our worst behavior; the flesh has the capacity to produce some admirable behavior. In fact; the flesh is the nature that is inherent in fallen humanity ..._even before_ behavior of any kind is undertaken or observed. It is who we are, not just what we do.

Consider the good deeds that are undertaken by people in all walks of life; Christians and non-Christians alike are both capable of acts of kindness, just as Christians and non-Christians are also capable of selfishness.

Indeed the most visible evidence of a flesh-based life may be self-absorbed living, but it is equally possible for the flesh to demonstrate great restraint and careful living. In the end it comes down to the individual, some people live more decent lives than others. The observable measure of our selfishness is not the defining characteristic of the flesh; rather it is defined by our independence from God. Or to put it another way; we feed on our own capacity to craft a meaningful life - rather than simply enjoying, and feeding on, the life that flows from our union with God.

When Jesus said; "The Spirit gives life, the flesh counts for nothing" he was speaking of man's insatiable need to be his own source of life. Jesus clarified in no uncertain terms that we have nothing to bring to the table; only he can provide life, only he is life! – the flesh counts for nothing.

If we think that the flesh is simply bad behavior, then we allow satan the lie – we give him permission to direct us to a life that finds meaning in its own independent good living, rather than finding meaning in its union with Jesus.

The thing then, which defines the flesh, is not so much its behavior
- as the source from which it draws life.

Chapter 4.
Whose Idea Was The Law?

Most Christians I know would answer that it was God's idea.

God had a standard that he required his people to measure up to - *so that he could fellowship with them.* He gave them a list of 10 straight forward commandments that articulated in easy terms his expectations. It was a guidebook that reflected his own perfect character - so that humanity would have a Godly moral compass to follow.

The implication of the view I have just stated above, is that God is primarily concerned about how we live. It appears that he has spelled-out his expectations of our behavior so that we can satisfy his scrutinizing eye. He is holy, so he is demanding holiness from us. Of course we know that the holiness-bar is way too high for us to jump, so God also threw in a back-up plan – repentance, sacrifices, religious lives.

But why would God become obsessed with our behavior now, when it wasn't even on his screen back in the garden? Why would God go to so much trouble to spell-out the rules? It's like he had a divine personality crisis and decided to be judge instead of loving father. You could get the impression that he was just waiting for mankind to screw-up so he could hammer us with the law.

And most of all; why would Jesus tell us that the flesh counts for nothing / while the Father is telling us that we should get the flesh busy living by the rules?

It seems to me that we have missed something very important.

Could it be that it was the flesh's idea to have the law? Fallen humanity had put God in a corner – God had no option but to articulate the real scale of his holiness, so that the flesh would finally grasp the futility of its foolish experiment.

In effect God said; "If you are hell-bent on manufacturing your own worth, then this is the standard required". He was simply articulating for humanity what they had set for themselves. It wasn't by his choice that mankind determined to go in this direction - but now that they had made-up their minds, God clarified what such a life would look like.

This distinction is paramount.

Even back in the wilderness when Israel received the law through Moses, satan was enforcing the lie. "At last you have the legal means by which the flesh can count, you have forced God's hand and can hold him accountable - *you can earn your own way by keeping the rules*". You can be god for yourself; all that is required is that you self-generated virtue – you can do it.

And so the experiment continued.

God gave Israel about 1500 years to try out their master plan – it was a tragic litany of failures, disasters and defeats. Even when Christ appeared on the scene they were still hammering away at the law, attempting to marry the most poorly suited candidates – *'holiness' / 'and the godless nature of humanity'*. These two were as incompatible at night and day, yet the flesh was determined to make a go of it – and satan was happy to oblige with his favorite lie ever; *'the flesh counts – don't give up'*.

Why did mankind continue to listen to the lie after all that time? Because humanity had no concept or memory of the way it was back in the garden, we couldn't conceive of an alternative – so the lie remained imprinted on the hearts of men.

Hebrews 7:18 tells us; "the law made nothing perfect". Israel missed it – the law was given to bring them to the end of themselves, but instead they developed the most rigorous religious system imaginable. The law was intended to illustrate their need for God, but all they did was re-double the efforts of the flesh. Religion was their way of counterfeiting Adams union with God – the flesh had developed a system that sounded like godly fellowship, and looked like a godly union, but it was the epitome of evil because it gave the flesh hope - *when it had no hope at all.*

The only hope was that we be re-united with the Tree of Life – Christ himself.

The word 'religion' has a very broad application in the minds of most people, it seems to encompass anything to do with God, church, and spiritual living. The context I am using for the word is much narrower – 'religion is the practices of humanity to satisfy the expectations of a perfect God'. Religion in my view is the construct of the flesh – it is humankind's attempt to meet God on his own terms. This is entirely different to Christianity in its true form, or the fellowship of believers on earth.

> *In short; we can be Christian without being religious.*
> *Or to put it another way;*
> *we can be in union with God, without the help of the flesh.*

In this regard it is reasonable to say that religion is man's idea not God's. God's idea was a perfect union sustained by the flow of life from him to us. In contrast; religion is man's attempt to copy the original by the efforts of the flesh... it is a perpetuation of 'the flesh counts'.

In broad terms, Christianity today is in the grip of 'the flesh counts' thinking. It is the underlying premise that it uses to interpret everything... *and systemized religion is the result.* Christ gave us back the union with God that Adam initially enjoyed, but it can only be received as a gift without any contribution from man.

It is the divine dare; I dare you to believe that my salvation for you is that good. I dare you to let go of the security of finding meaning in what you do – *and find it in who you are… because of my love for you!*

When you do, life will overflow from you like a fountain – Christ within, bursting forth. The mysterious union known as 'Christ-within' will produce good living all by itself.

Chapter 5.
Why Did Christ Come?

That's easy; Christ came to pay for our sins, he came to give us life, he came to destroy the works of the enemy.

These answers roll off our tongue with relative ease, they are the information we have based our faith on – everyone agrees with this.

The information is certainly not faulty; rather, it is the foundational thinking that we hold, that carries this information - which is often at fault. We come with a nature that is pre-wired to interpret everything through the lens 'the flesh counts', it is this pre-disposition that leads us to very wrong conclusions about 'why Christ came'.

We are pre-wired with the notion that the problem with human-kind is that we sin. In reality this is merely the fruit of a much greater problem – that we are independent from God. This independence from God causes us to sin; and it also causes us to attempt to be the solution.

Not that we directly attempt to be our own savior and pay the price of our sins - but that having received salvation, we subsequently attempt to maintain our fellowship with God through a God-pleasing life. Our flesh-nature is content enough to receive forgiveness from the death and resurrection of Christ, but it is very reluctant to accept that Christ has also re-built our union with God. Our flesh is determined to make this 'relationship maintenance' role its own task – it is determined to engage all of its own resources in the construction of a God-pleasing life – *it is determined that the role of the flesh counts.*

Like the nation of Israel of old; our flesh-nature feels most at home when it has a list to follow, boxes to tick, and religion to practice – it has been pre-wired to do this ever since it took leave of God's life-giving presence on that tragic day in the garden.

So why did Christ come? Sure he came to pay the penalty for our sins – this was like picking all of the fruit from our sin-laden tree. But what then of the tree itself? It would simply grow more fruit and become as sin-laden as it was in the start. The flesh constructed a convenient solution for this; it decided to give itself the role of confessing every sin it committed post-salvation, to keep in God's good books.

> *This is classic 'the flesh counts' stuff…*
> **God does his bit / we do our bit**
> **– everyone is happy!**

But God wouldn't have it. His solution was far more robust that depending on the flesh to measure-up, it hadn't managed to measure-up for millennia, *why would it succeed now.*

God's solution was so radical that it took satan by complete surprise. Instead of leaving humanity with a lifelong maintenance role, Christ did the unthinkable – he crucified the flesh-nature of man within his own crucifixion. He took the self-based nature of the flesh and crucified it with himself, in his own death.

Our sinful nature ceased to exist in the instant we received Christ. Paul says in Colossians 3:3 "For you died, and your life is now hidden with Christ in God".

The lie from satan is this; 'we were not crucified at all - we still have God-pleasing work to do'.

Chapter 5. Why Did Christ Come?

If all Christ did was forgive our sins - then we remain locked in a life-long obligation to maintain relationship with God through a life of good deeds and religious practices. If on the other hand Christ also crucified our fallen-nature, then we have truly been set free. Free to be in our original status of perfect union with God, and to live great lives in the Spirit without any regard for the obligations of the flesh.

Free to live in the Spirit, with scant regard for the self-righteousness motivated, compulsive works of the flesh.

In 2 Corinthians 5:21 Paul says; "God made him who had no sin to be sin for us, so that in him we might become the righteousness of God". Christ became sin, so that we might become righteousness. This is more than just the payment of a debt, this is the exchange of two natures – he took our sinful flesh nature, and exchanged it with his own righteous divine nature. Christ did not become sins (plural), he became sin – he became the rebellious, independent nature of humanity that we might become the container of the nature of God.

Is this too good?

I hope so… if the salvation of Christ is not too good to be true – then it probably isn't true. This is the one thing that Paul spoke of, it is the pearl of great price – it is the true gospel without the pull of the flesh.

Christ not only picked all of the fruit from our sin-bearing tree, he also put the axe to it, and cut it out roots and all. He destroyed the independent Godless existence which is the flesh-nature, and re-birthed us as the twice born ones – those born again with the very nature of God.

This gospel doesn't get much air-play around Christian circles; we don't by nature know how to be in a union with God that requires no contribution from us. It eludes us to conceive of a form of Christianity that has no strings attached. It has been so long since humans lived in the Garden of God that we have no instinct about how to make it work, and so we automatically default to 'The Flesh Counts' thinking.

It's not that we believers aren't saved; it's just that we don't know how to 'walk in the Spirit' because of our pre-disposition towards walking in the flesh. The fact is that the flesh has nothing at all to bring to the table; all we have to offer is belief that God could love us so much – *and even that, we do only by his grace.*

Satan's lie is like an echo from our old nature, ringing in our ears… 'The flesh counts'.

The flesh-nature is long dead; yet day-in, day-out, satan whispers his old lie to the hearts of well-meaning Christians the world over, "The Flesh Counts, keep up the good work".

The tragedy is that Christ paid such a high price for our freedom from 'the bondage to self-generate security', a freedom that was intended to begin in the instant we turned to Christ and received his love. But instead, satan has managed to keep far too many believers from their inheritance as God's sons and daughters in the here and now, settling to only partake of it fully after we die.

> **We have been made into the King's offspring,**
> **but instead have chosen mere servitude in its place.**

You might be thinking; "my motivation to 'live right' is not to establish my security, but to lead a responsible Christian life" – the test is whether we can stand naked of all our good deeds and lifestyle before the throne of God, in full confidence that God accepts us on the merits of Christ's blood, independent of any good we may do. This bare-faced confidence in Christ is rare these days; we are more likely to observe a well-crafted mix of Christ + us.

In so doing we perpetuate the legacy of Adam, he placed his own goodness along-side Gods – and the fallen nature of humanity was the result.

Christ came to crucify the fallen nature of humanity.

Chapter 5. Why Did Christ Come?

Unfortunately, humanity does not want a gospel that crucifies our fallen nature; it would rather that our old nature be alive and kicking, so that it can get on with wrestling with it. Humanity would prefer that we have two natures side by side (the sin-nature and the born-again nature), – this then gives the individual a mission, a purpose, and a role - it wants to overcome the flesh, and be validated for it.

God knew how humanity would respond, he didn't ask for anyone's permission; he just went ahead and crucified the flesh; because if it remained alive it would continue to usurp his role as 'Life Provider'. He denied the flesh any part in the matter – and gave us back the divine life-source that we started with, at absolutely no cost to us. Satan's lie is to convince us that the flesh remains alive, and has a critical role to play.

Satan knows that if he can keep our eyes fixed on our own good living and religious practices – we will not enter into that far superior life known as 'walking in the Spirit'. It's a life where the presence of Christ-within produces goodness as we rest in his power, his nature, and his love.

> *It is essential that we understand*
> *that God is not opposed to a life of good works,*
> *but that these good works must be the result of a life*
> *that looks to Christ as the engine room for this goodness,*
> *rather than itself.*

When the source is Christ – then the Spirit is everything / when the source is self-generated – then the flesh counts. When we feed on the Tree of Life – goodness appears from God's nature within us. When we feed on the Tree that attempts to generate life out of its own juggling of good and evil – sin appears from our fallen nature.

Can you see the difference?

Chapter 6.
Religion V. Faith.

ONE of my favorite chapters in the bible is the first chapter of Ephesians. Paul wrote his letter to this church without addressing any particular heresy or error. They were a church that had a good grasp on their salvation - so Paul set about expanding their horizons from this solid base. He wanted them to see more, and further, into the realm of God.

In Ephesians 1:17 Paul prays a prayer for them that comes out of left field. Instead of asking God to do something for the Ephesians; (equip them for ministry, or bless them in some way) - he asks God to show them something. He prays that 'the eyes of their hearts would be enlightened' so they might grasp the scale of their salvation.

In effect Paul is showing us that we do not lack Gods involvement in our lives - we lack the ability to see the scale of how much he is already involved.

It is this 'sight' that swings the pendulum from 'the flesh counts' to 'the Spirit gives life'. If we cannot see our new nature with clarity, then we will be inclined to personally engage ourselves in the process of getting God involved in the issues of *our* life. If we can see that God is so involved in us that he has actually made his home in us, then we cease trying to get him involved - *and rest in his presence.*

Religion tries to get God involved,
Faith declares God is involved already.

Religion activates the flesh to call forth God's help through various activities, practices and lifestyle. Faith declares there is nothing I need to do to activate God's help, he has already made provision for all that my heart desires - all I need to do is believe him, and rest in him.

Religion declares that 'the flesh counts'. It declares that God cannot respond to us if we are not living a lifestyle of Christian activity, good deeds, and godly thoughts. Religious people are most secure when they are most busy in the tasks of Christianity.

Faith declares the opposite, 'the flesh counts for nothing'. It declares that God responds to us as we rest in the person and work of Jesus Christ. It is Christ's 'life-giving' activities that attract God's favor, not our own. People of faith are secure because they have viewed the grandeur of Christ, and lean into his goodness.

Paul was not especially concerned with the lifestyle or good deeds of the Ephesian church – he just wanted to extend their vision beyond its present horizon. He wanted to expose them to more of Christ, because the more they grasped the stunning work that he completed for them, the more they would live magnificent lives in the power of the Spirit.

His desire was that they would gain their identity from Christ – not from their religious activities. He wanted them to see that the revelation of Christ is everything, and even the most impressive activities *(read: worship leading, preaching, witnessing)* do not rate by comparison.

All of this is perfectly clear to satan… he just doesn't want it to be clear to us.

For this reason satan promotes the flesh with his classic lie. He tells the flesh what it loves to hear – that it is important, that it has a vital role to play, and that God wants its contribution. He tells us that God is watching and waiting for us to live-out a life in imitation of Christ, that it is what we were made for.

CHAPTER 6. RELIGION V. FAITH.

We were not made for imitation; we were made for the original – Christ living in us.

He is more than an example for us to follow; he is the in-dwelling God who lives his life through us.

Satan does not attempt anything as obvious as suggesting that God doesn't love us – we would see that coming a mile off. Instead he tells us that God is keeping something from us, something that we are entitled to have – 'The Knowledge of Good and Evil'.

As soon as this knowledge is ours, the flesh has its chance – it can construct a life based on the merits of its own handling of good and evil, then the flesh can become our life-source, instead of the Spirit.

This is why Christ came – to give us life, *'the Spirit gives life'*.

John 10:10 says "I came that they may have life, and have it abundantly". This is not referring to the needs of the natural realm; it is saying that he came to give life back to our dead spirit – the life that the flesh took from us. He came to breathe the life of his Spirit back in to our own deceased spirit, so that he could move back in, and fill us with his nature again.

This becomes a fact in the instant we receive salvation; we may not perceive it physically, but it is none-the-less completely true. Satan cannot steal this away from us, he cannot re-kill that which Christ has made alive – but he can deceive us into living a life that robs us of the reality of it, until we close our eyes at our physical death.

This is satan's goal; to keep us from enjoying our inheritance for as long as possible. He does this by convincing us that the flesh *(our self-motivated goodness)* is our source of life, rather than the Spirit of Christ.

Religion is the perpetuation of the first lie, the one told long ago in the Garden of Eden. Its sole aim is to keep us from our God-given identity as his sons and daughters, and relegate us to the status of servants - *those who find meaning in the tasks they perform / rather than the family they are a part of.* Their value is measured by their conduct, rather than by their heritage – they have chosen the flesh over the Spirit.

It is this need to find our identity in ourselves and our actions - which is the fodder for Satan's lies.

Chapter 7.
The Battle For Our Minds.

Every human being born on the planet since Adam and Eve has had a mindset that is naturally drawn towards finding security and identity in their own actions. This is the lie written into our fallen nature. Christ himself is the only exception – his security and identity was entirely based on the love relationship between himself and his Father.

Every human being from the earliest days until now has tried to find his/her identity in the way he/she lives their life. Be it; the practice of religion, hard work, acts of charity, or any other lifestyle we may choose – we are wired-up to feel safest, and happiest, when we have done our part.

It is deeply programmed into our make-up, and it is so universally accepted, that we consider it the normal human condition – *and indeed it is the normal condition of the fallen nature.* It is part of the package deal that came with Adam's desertion from the kingdom of God. The currency of the kingdom of God is God's divine life flowing through us for free - the currency of the kingdom of darkness is self-made life.

Every human being since Adam and Eve has been born into the kingdom of darkness. Even though satan poses as an angel of light, he remains the ruler of darkness – he presents an attractive kingdom view to any un-witting human being who is seeking identity through their own actions, he gives them a stage upon which to construct their identity. The world validates humanity for achievement and effort, it applauds our milestones – *and satan is also happy, just so long as our focus is on ourselves.*

He presents the eager human being with the opportunity to find their identity on the world stage, and we are drawn to it like a moth to a flame because it is our nature to do so. It seems we are helpless *(and indeed we are, were it not for Christ)* but to find meaning in our lives through our conduct and achievements, according to our earthly performance. Satan writes the script, directs, and produces the show – and a world full of well-intentioned people find security, meaning, and identity in their own actions.

When we received salvation Christ tore-up the old script. The curtain came down for the last time on the longest running show in human history – "The Flesh Counts".

Jesus wrote a new production called "Life in the Spirit" – it's the only show in town now.

All the old theatres have long-since shut down, they are boarded-up and but a dim memory of their former glory. Yet, day-after-day Christians push their way into the old theatre and act-out the old script, attempting to find meaning in all the old lines, putting-in their best performance with all their hearts.

Worst of all, satan applauds their efforts and the drama continues. He yells his affirmation to the enthusiastic players from the sidelines – "The flesh counts, keep up the good work, the show must go on".

Does it have to be this way?

Can we escape the vicious cycle and join the new script? Can we leave behind a way of life that has become so in-grained that it fits like our favorite old shoes?

The answer is a resounding YES!

There is a price!

Chapter 7. The Battle For Our Minds.

Not a price in human effort, sacrifice or personal cost… the price is to let go of the earthly props that have sustained us thus far, and cast ourselves with full abandon into the goodness of God, resting in his ability alone to hold us and keep us.

In a sense the price we pay is everything, everything that has provided for our identity and security so far. This is no small thing because the echo of our old nature continues to reverberate around our minds, pulling us into our old ways of thinking – yet we were re-born for this new life, we were re-born to be safely home in God - *with the thinking of the flesh just a dim memory.*

This is the final battleground for satan – the mind of the born-again believer.

Satan suffered the most crushing defeat imaginable at the cross of Christ; now he slinks around the shadows, whispering lies in the hope that human beings will fall for his deceit and begin to doubt their true nature in Christ.

He fears us - just as he fears Christ himself.

He fears that we will grasp our new identity and flick him off like an annoying bug. He knows that he is completely subject to our commands and authority, and must obey us without reservation – his deceit is aimed at obscuring from our view the true status which is ours in Christ. If he can do that then he can continue to carry on his foolish mission.

He knows that he is powerless to resist the presence of Christ within us; he just doesn't want us to be aware of it. His strategy is to convince Christians that Christ has only gone part-way and that the flesh must play its part for victory to be gained – he knows that if we discover the truth he will be crushed under our feet. Because while he has us focused on our own religious activity, we will never be able to fully abandon ourselves to the accomplishments of the cross of Christ.

If we gain a clear view of who we truly are – satan's cause is over, and he is finally seen for what he is, the biggest fool in the history of creation. He doesn't even care if we rise-up and fight him, he just doesn't want us to realize he is already beaten. He doesn't want us to rest in the victory of the cross of Christ, he would rather we raise-up our flesh against him. He doesn't care if we throw ourselves into any and every type of spiritual warfare – we can yell, jump and make all the demands we like… *as long as we don't rest in the sufficiency of Christ.*

**He knows the flesh counts for nothing
– he just doesn't want us to know it.**

And that is the nub of it!

Satan doesn't care two-hoots if we are the most religiously zealous, dedicated, faithful, good-living Christian man or woman to ever walk the face of the earth. He doesn't care if we are the biggest giver, the most tireless evangelist, or the most sacrificial missionary in history - as long as we do these things out of a sense of obligation and sacrificial duty, energized by the motivations of the flesh.

If on the other hand we discover that 'one thing' that Paul knew, and embark on the most restful, yet fruitful life imaginable, then satan is crushed under our feet.

*All because we stopped trying to be
- what Christ has already made us into.*

Paul made a remarkable statement in Romans 14:23 "That which is not of faith, is sin", it effectively means the same thing as the statement Jesus made in John 6:63 "The Spirit gives life, the flesh counts for nothing".

My paraphrase: The Life of the Spirit produces spontaneous faith / the flesh produces works that are worth nothing, which are in fact 'sin' when we look to them for our security and identity.

Chapter 7. The Battle For Our Minds.

These two scriptures are aimed squarely at the lie that is written on the hearts of humankind, they have the potential to dismantle the lie and launch us into Life in the Spirit – but only if we let go of our dependence on the works of the flesh to provide our sense of security.

We might work tirelessly in our local soup kitchen, we might be a champion of the cause of the down trodden – but these do not define us as Christian, only faith in the blood of Christ can do that. Yet as a community, we Christians are more comfortable in our acts of charity, than in hiding ourselves in the sacrifice of Christ.

The challenge for us here is that the lie is us. Before coming to Christ – 'we and the lie' were inextricably linked. And even after coming to Christ its image lingers in the un-renewed mind.

It is like a photograph that is indelibly imprinted into our mind, it is always there – no mental exercise or therapy can erase it. Just as we can never separate ourselves from the mental image of a loved one – we cannot separate ourselves from the deeply-rooted lie we love, which is written on our hearts.

Why? Because this lie makes us tick. It is in-back of everything that defines who we are; it is inconceivable to imagine life without it.

It is the lie we like best - because we are one with it,
it is our legacy from Adam.

Paul articulates the only way out so clearly in Galatians 2:20 "I have been crucified with Christ, I no longer live but Christ lives in me". Paul is telling us that the only way to dispose of the lie – is to acknowledge that Christ has crucified the heart that harbors it. Then a new man can come forth who has a new statement written on his heart "The Spirit gives life", this new man is the mystery hidden for ages and now revealed to us 'Christ in me'.

Now the Spirit can declare at last; "no longer are you and the lie one / now you and Christ are one".

Chapter 8.
We Must Die Before We Can Live.

Paul described a type of death in many of his letters, a death that is different to the end of our physical lives:

Galatians 2:20 – "I have been crucified with Christ, I no longer live…"

Colossians 3:3 – "For you died, and your life is now hidden with Christ in God".

Romans 6:6 – "For we know that our old self was crucified with him…"

2 Corinthians 5:14 – "we are convinced that one died for all, and therefore all died".

This death is clearly not the one where we take our last breath and pass from this life, it is a death that is spiritual not physical. This spiritual death is the reason why Christ came – to crucify the nature that became humanity's when Adam and Eve rebelled. He came to undo the lie (to kill it), and give us his own life in its place.

We do not crucify our flesh, Christ does.

The scriptures tell us that before we came to Christ we were 'dead to God, but alive to sin'. This life within us was our sinful nature (or flesh), it became alive when Adam and Eve walked away from their union with God – it was a life that was nourished by the self-sustaining efforts of the flesh.

It was a vicious cycle. A cycle that fed upon the flesh's juggling of good & evil to keep it alive. There was no capacity to escape the vicious cycle because the sinful nature had given up its ability to rest in the nourishment of the love of God – the flesh had nowhere to go but to continue striving to build its worth from within itself.

All the flesh could do was apply itself to the task of forming value from its own deeds (good or bad). It had no hope because true worth can only be found in the heart of God - all it could do was attempt to fabricate a copy, self-made worth / instead of God-given worth.

Only God could resolve the problem – humanity had nothing to bring to the table.

God couldn't simply choose to accept humankind back on their own terms, (light and darkness cannot mix; holiness and sin cannot fellowship together). The only way a re-union could be brokered was that God would have to enact a hostage exchange – *Jesus would have to become humanity, so that we could become divinity.* For this to take place a complete transfer would be necessary – all that defines our flesh nature, would be exchanged for all that defines his divine nature.

Christ became sin, and we became the righteousness of God.

He became us – and we became him.

Then he suffered our punishment…

And when it was done he burst free – his righteousness was indestructible. As he came up out of that place of punishment he 'took captivity captive' – he conquered the age-old enemies of humanity 'sin, death, and hell' – and we were returned to the original design.

Christ has destroyed the Old Nature – he has completed his mission. And now he gives all of humanity the right to become sons and daughters of God – our only part is to believe that he could be so good, and say "Yes" to him.

Chapter 8. We Must Die Before We Can Live.

Everyone who says "Yes" is carried through Christ's crucifixion and into his righteousness. Every human being who is 'born again' has had his 'Old Nature' crucified. It is not an optional extra, or a task that we apply ourselves to subsequent to receiving salvation – it is simply a fact.

To be Born Again - and to have our Old Nature crucified with Christ, are synonymous – they are exactly the same event.

It is a spiritual event that was completed in its entirety by Christ – there is not a Christian on planet earth who has not been crucified with Christ.

There are however, many Christians who have no idea that the death of their Old Nature came as part of the package. They continue trying to keep the 10 commandments (or whatever code of behavior they choose) to please God and obtain his blessings. They do not understand that this spiritual death took place in them, and so they continue to live as if the Old Nature and all of its obligations remains alive and intact. They don't grasp that Christ came to set them free from the flesh, and so they live a lie – instead of being 'free indeed' they live as a captive.

Christ paid for their freedom, *there is no outstanding debt* – yet, their lack of understanding traps them within the very lie that Christ came to destroy.

In effect, they live as one who is without Christ – *until they leave this life and discover what they have had all along.* There is no question that they are in every way complete in their salvation, but their lack of knowledge robs them of it in the 'here and now'.

While they live out their remaining days on planet earth they fail to profoundly take part in the very thing that Christ accomplished (the destruction of their Old Nature), and so their lives are barely distinguishable from the unsaved - *but for the visible practice of religion.*

Many would find these words too strong, suggesting that they are doing their best (as well as anyone else is doing) – and that is the point, it is not what we do that releases us into the amazing benefits that are ours because of the cross of Christ - *but rather the truth that we have seen, and believe in.*

There is no alternative way that Christ offers to the vast congregation of Christianity. He does not craft a salvation especially designed for those who wish to find security on their own terms – he offers us a choice 'die with him, or live without him'.

It's a sad paradox that Christians can have so much, yet realize so little. When we physically die we will grasp in the blink of an eye the vast transformation that was wrought in us by the cross of Christ. We will see at the end of our earthly journey what has actually been our true self for the whole time – but it will be too late, we will have crossed over into eternity, and the earthly adventure of faith will have passed us by.

We will see that Christ did indeed crucify our flesh, he did indeed do away with our old nature – yet for many they lived out their years on the planet as only a small fraction of the person he had made them, *all for the lack of knowledge.*

For the vast majority eternity began years ago, perhaps decades ago (when they first received Christ as savior) – but many only truly grasp the wonder of it when the final curtain comes down, and it is all over.

They were dead – they just didn't know it!

There is nothing lacking in the work of Christ. His crucifixion work was concluded in every way – our old flesh nature was nailed to his cross as certain as Christ's own flesh was pinned there, until he breathed his final breath – *and it was done.* The only thing lacking is our knowledge of that fact, and our willingness to live our lives with that as our deepest truth.

Beyond death there is life. Mortality gives way to immortality. The earth is merely a waiting room for our new life in heaven.

But when do we possess it?

Chapter 8. We Must Die Before We Can Live.

John 5:24 says that we <u>have</u> crossed over from death to life; it is present tense not future tense.

Could it be that we choose?

The journey from 'death to life' is the inheritance of every believer. Our 'dead to God' spirits are revived to 'new life in eternity' when we pass out of this earthly realm – *but is it possible for us to bring forward the reality of that event into the present day?*

The death of our old nature has been completed by Christ in every way, all that remains is that we agree with this truth, and live out the days we have left as *'those who started eternity early'*. It's in our hands, we can delay the 'wonders of eternity' until our physical death if we like, or we can have them now – we can choose our own reality.

> *It is our gift from Christ – we can un-wrap it when we like,*
> *it is up to us!*

All of eternity is ours, we are home – all that stands in our way is the insistence of the flesh that we remain self-fed, instead of resting in Christ's ability to nourish us with his spiritual life. If we cease to be spiritually nourished by our self-generated sense of worth – then eternity starts early! John 5:24 says; "Very truly I tell you, whoever hears my word and believes him who sent me <u>has eternal life</u> and will not be judged but <u>has crossed over from death to life</u>".

That statement may sound a bit vague; it seems unlikely that we can gain eternity *(perhaps decades early)* by simply adjusting our thinking – *and that is where death comes in.* It is more than an adjustment; it is the end of life as we know it.

For the majority of Christians life is a drawn-out process of overcoming the weaknesses of the flesh. It is a battle that begins anew each day as we determine to live better, wiser and godlier lives. It is a cycle of self-improvement

that records little (if any) progress, and is finally concluded when we step off the treadmill of self-development on the day we die.

There is no doubt that there lays dormant within each of us the potential for self-improvement. We each have the capacity to live better lives, defined by the visible evidence of good behavior and lifestyle.

It is the security we place in this 'self-constructed worth' that determines whether we arrive in eternity early. In fact, it is the perpetuation of this 'self-improvement process' that gives life to the lie. The lie dies when we lift our eyes off our own performance and behavior, and onto Christ.

We take all of the eggs that were previously distributed over our many self-based undertakings, and place them all into Christ's basket – he becomes our entire satisfaction and source of worth.

Even the really good eggs like bible study, prayer, worship, and charity, have no inherent worth in them – if we do not grasp first, that our worth is complete without them, *because of Christ.*

Dare we stand naked before God (just as Adam and Eve did at the start), confident that our standing is established by Christ's virtue alone, confident that God is 100% satisfied with us - *even if (perish the thought) we do nothing for him.*

When we can do that; when we are so bold as to declare "Christ was enough for me" – then the death of the flesh is truly ours, and eternity can begin – *the adventure of life in the Spirit has started.* We don't have to wait for heaven; it has made its home in us *even though we remain on earth* – with the result that works of life burst forth from our new eternal nature.

There are some who think that Jesus stands at the door of heaven, welcoming home the faithful when they die, and presenting them with their 'Crown of Life'. There are others who think that Jesus welcomed them home on the day they were saved - and since then Jesus has regarded them as citizens of heaven who have been wearing the 'Crown of Life' even though they remained on earth.

I subscribe to the second group... what about you?

Chapter 9.
Putting 'No Confidence' In The Flesh.

From time to time we hear in politics or business that a 'no confidence' vote was taken against a particular leader or group. In our part of the world a local Town Council was recently removed by the State Government because they had become dysfunctional and self-serving. The government opted to wipe the slate clean and put all positions up for re-election, rather than retain any of the existing Councilors.

This particular Town Council was experiencing such infighting and poor performance that they were all sacked; there wasn't a redeeming quality amongst them. Even though the Town Council had been duly elected by the people, and made significant promises during the election campaign – even though they had great potential for good, and were liked by many - the State Government expressed 'no confidence' and chose to start afresh.

It is this 'no confidence' which is at the heart of Paul's statement in Philippians 3:3 "we who serve God by his Spirit, who boast in Christ Jesus, and who put no confidence in the flesh".

Paul is saying that "the flesh can't do the job". Even though we may consider it has great potential and holds great promise – it simply isn't up to the task of making any spiritual contribution. God doesn't hold out any hope that the flesh might come through, he confirmed his vote of 'no confidence' when he sent Jesus to the cross 2000 years ago. In fact, he knew at the beginning that humanity's crazy experiment with the Tree of the Knowledge of Good and Evil would prove to be a disaster.

Back in chapter 3, I defined 'the flesh' in this way; it is the nature of man / without the life giving righteousness of God to keep it. It is not our body, or our physical self – but rather it is our true self that lies beneath the physical, in the realm of the spirit. It is the self-based substance of humanity that has not died to allow the life-giving nature of Christ to take its place. It is the fallen nature of humanity saying "I can do it" even though God has cast his vote against it.

Many believers will give their nod of approval to this definition, yet the majority have not truly grasped the full substance of it. This definition has implicit within it, a radical shift of thinking that the majority shy away from – God doesn't want our personal best, he wants us to stop trying so hard - and simply hold-on to Jesus.

The notion that God is not interested in our best attempts to live right, is a step too-far for many believers. They are convinced that God is conducting a thorough observation of how we are doing, and that his tick of approval is our reward. It would be reckless beyond reason to contemplate any alternative – yet it is this mindset that holds most believers in the realm of the flesh, when they should be letting the ambitions of the old nature die, so that Life in the Spirit can begin.

These are not overlapping circles;
our best + Jesus best = God's approval.

The best intentions of man do not mesh with the work of the Spirit – Christ has done it all. Our best intentions are irrelevant until we have cast ourselves fully into the gift of Christ, (*without even contemplating any kind of response*). Until then our response is nothing more than filthy rags, motivated by the faithless conscience of humanity.

Chapter 9. Putting 'No Confidence' In The Flesh.

Does this sound too harsh – I hope so!

This gospel is radical beyond description, Jesus takes you home for free, he invites you to come to the great banquet and provides the transport as well – he doesn't even care if you are not good enough, because his goodness is enough for everyone.

In fact, let's take it a step further – he <u>wants</u> you to be 'not good enough' because with that realization we will at last stop trying to qualify, and start resting in his qualification. This sentiment reflects perfectly the correct understanding of 'no confidence'.

In contrast, our 'confidence' should be equivalent to the smelliest, drunken derelict staggering up to the throne of God and boldly declaring "I'm with him" *(Jesus)* – we bring no personal value to the matter.

Modern Christianity has made such a doctrine out of the believer's need to present God with a righteous life, that we don't know how to come to him anymore when we are devoid of such trappings. We are insecure about our standing with God if we haven't read the word, prayed, and worshiped consistently. Yet these things don't qualify us to stand boldly before the throne of God, only the blood of Christ does that.

> ***When you break it down; we have more faith in our own right living – than we do in the blood of Christ.***

Or to put it another way; we put our confidence in our own flesh – instead of Jesus.

As I mentioned earlier; our right living / and Christ's sacrifice - do not combine to make a well balanced Christian life. They are mutually exclusive elements. Right living springs forth like a fountain welling-up from within us, as a result of fixing our gaze on Jesus alone.

It is perhaps the greatest error preached in the vast majority of churches today – "that believers are exhorted to produce a life of good deeds and service, in response to Christ's example". Christ didn't come to be our example; he came to kill the nature that is determined to craft a copy of his life – so that he could move in, and produce the life that is truly pleasing to God, through his own Godly nature.

> *In short: God doesn't want our best efforts*
> *– he wants Christ's life flowing through us.*

The message that churches need Sunday after Sunday is; 'Christ has done it all'. We need to train the flock to fix their eyes on Jesus. We need to teach people how to be confident in his blood – then works of life will appear. The more people are told how to live, the more they put confidence in the flesh. The more there are directed to Jesus / the more his goodness appears, just like fruit on a vine.

It defies our deepest instincts to promote such a gospel. The lie that 'the flesh counts' is written so indelibly into our hearts that we default to it, without even considering whether it is right. It is the reason why Jesus had to give us a spiritual heart transplant – the old one was beyond repair, it was too damaged by a lifelong diet from the wrong tree – so it had to be torn out and replaced with his own.

This makes the lie that satan promotes all the more insidious – he convinces the masses that their old heart is still operational, and with a little extra effort we can get it functioning again. He convinces us that Christ is in the *heart-patching-up* business, that he values our efforts to pump out goodness – and wants to work with us to get the old unit back into useful production again.

Nothing could be further from the truth.

Even King David back in the Old Testament understood this when he prayed that God would 'create within him a new heart'. We are on the other side of the cross from David, we have been given the new heart that he longed for – how sad that many prefer to try to kick-start the old one, instead of resting in the new one to do more than we have ever thought or dreamt possible.

Chapter 10.
The Heart Transplant We Had To Have.

As the revelation of the scale and substance of my salvation has dawned upon me, I have found myself reflecting on the sad state of my previous perceptions of the work of Christ. The unlimited wonder and potential of my re-born nature was largely concealed by earth-bound reasoning, with the result that my salvation was more of a collection of spiritual opinions and doctrines – than a dynamic life in the Spirit.

I was not deliberately diminishing my understanding of the accomplishments of Christ, but rather was constrained within the well-crafted reasoning of religion. It seemed that I had no internal capacity to see beyond the physical realm – I was stuck in Adam's post-Eden systematic thinking.

This systematic thinking had an inbuilt mechanism which always looked for the human trigger that was necessary to access the divine realm. It was pre-programmed to seek out the process God required of me - to release his favor, blessing, or peace into my circumstances. Or conversely; my sinful living had caused God to remove his favor, opening the way for sickness, poverty, or strife.

In regard to reading Gods word, this post-Eden mind always looked for a formula, system, or activity. It would automatically zero-in on 'what God required of me' so that his loving response could flow my way. It looked for principles that could be employed as the channels through which blessing could be gained.

Take for instance 'financial blessing'. My systematic mind was focused on getting the necessary environment in order, so that God could do what I needed him to do – *bless me*. This meant that I should tithe at least one tenth of my income, become a generous hearted person, and exercise good financial management and restraint – with these principles in place I would be well positioned for God's blessing to flow, (and by default, if they weren't in place, then I was out of position to receive his favor).

In back of this thinking was the notion that Jesus had removed the sin barrier between me and God, which enabled me to access God's favor by a life based on good principles and choices. It was a mindset that meshed the work of Christ, with my good and principled living – like a well-oiled machine, the gears of Christ's sacrifice / and my response, meshed together to generate a favorable outcome.

Without realizing it, I was attempting to participate in the work of the cross with the very thinking that had made the cross necessary in the first place. I was bringing my own virtuous life alongside Christ's life to open the way to blessing – which was no different to Adam's approach.

The reason I did this is that one foundational assumption governed my thinking – 'God required me to be good'. His favor was directly linked to my behavior.

This assumption was based on the notion that God was pleased with Adam *(before he sinned)* because he lived a good life that God found acceptable, and that subsequently God was displeased with Adam (and all of humanity) because the sinful nature had inhibited their ability to live an acceptable life. It followed then, that the reason why Christ came, was to pay our sin debt - so that we could once again live a life that God would find acceptable.

This assumption had shaped my faith into an *'acceptable-lifestyle based'* belief system.

Such a belief system has taken the lavish, generosity of God and constrained it within the self-obsessed systems of fallen humanity – with the outcome

Chapter 10. The Heart Transplant We Had To Have.

that we are by nature incapable of receiving from God without the benefit of some human action, lifestyle or principle.

The reason why God doesn't want us to <u>be</u> good, is that the blood of Christ has already <u>made us</u> good. There is nothing I can do to add to the good nature that Christ gave me – I am perfectly good quite apart from my earthly lifestyle choices. When I grasp this truth, Christ's goodness is expressed through my life. If, on the other hand, I do not grasp this truth, then all of my efforts to please God through good living are worth no more than dirty laundry.

God provided the most elegantly logical solution to the problem. He would remove from us the old heart that was incapable of understanding the ways of the Spirit, and replace it with his own heart that was completely at home in the realm of the Spirit.

This new heart is not the blood pumping device that keeps our physical body alive, it is the life of Christ within us that keeps our spirit alive to God. Sometimes it is referred to as the inner man, sometimes our spirit, or the heart of man – it refers to our true self, which resides within the physical man.

The heart of man no longer harbors the lie, it parted company with the lie when Christ took up residence within us – *light and darkness cannot co-exist*. But the lie continues to echo around our minds until we deliberately arrest its presence, and replace it with thinking that is in keeping with the truth.

Christ gives us a new heart,
and we must bring our mind into agreement with it.

Romans 12:2 is probably the clearest explanation of this process; "be transformed by the renewing of your mind". The Romans were clearly a congregation of believers who had the nature of Christ as their new identity, yet Paul exhorts them to be transformed by the renewing of their minds. A further transformation was possible for them that involved a deeper way of grasping the truth. Their hearts had been renewed by Christ, and now Paul urged them to bring their thinking into agreement with that transformation.

If this 'mind renewing' does not take place, then we remain people who apply the fallen thinking of Adam as we attempt to apprehend the redeemed life which is ours in Christ.

The fallen thinking of Adam is that God wants my Christian walk to be based on an acceptable lifestyle. In contrast, renewed thinking understands that Christ has redeemed me from the tyranny of performance-based Christianity, into Spirit energized life.

These two are opposites.

The ultimate outcome of applying an un-renewed mind in attempting to understand spiritual things is that we perceive spiritual reality according to Adam's point of view – which means we view our salvation from the perspective of the flesh instead of the Spirit.

Unfortunately we are by nature very attached to our old heart and the way it views life, we like the lie it tells us because it gives us the feedback we have come to love – 'that we are doing a good job'.

It is our attachment to our old heart that keeps us from perceiving the spiritual landscape that is our real inheritance in Christ. It holds us in our limited earth-bound perceptions, when the reality of our identity in Christ is immeasurably more. We are made of the same spiritual genetics as Christ himself – but our attachment to the old ways keeps us functioning as men and women of mere flesh.

The un-renewed mind has a unique method that it applies to the revelation of 'Christ in us' and the resulting transformation – it does not deny the truth, in fact it gives it a polite nod of approval, but then proceeds to fit this information into its established paradigms. Instead of elevating the revelation of Christ to its proper place and making changes accordingly, it places the revelation of Christ into subservience to flesh - with the result that our Christianity resembles Adam's way of life more than Christ's.

Chapter 10. The Heart Transplant We Had To Have.

The lie hides from us our true identity.

This is probably starting to sound like a stuck record that goes over and over the same track, and indeed it is - because every way we look at the problem of the flesh we end up back where we started, stuck in a track that we are incapable of lifting ourselves out of.

It is the sad dilemma of humanity; that so few will ever go beyond the limitations of the flesh and be carried aloft by the breath of the Spirit of God - all for the lack of knowledge.

It is the reason why Jesus made that extraordinary statement in Luke 18:8 "However, when the Son of Man comes, will he find faith on the earth?" It is not a question of whether the earth is heavily populated by Christians, but whether these Christians have grasped what they have within them – *and allowed themselves to be transformed by it.*

It would be unthinkable to imagine a heart transplant patient who chooses to remain bed-ridden for the rest of their life after receiving their new heart. The whole point of the operation was to open the way for a vibrant new life. Yet many Christians have been given a new heart from Christ and choose to remain within the limited conditions of the old one – all because they don't realize it has taken place.

Our identity has been translated out of the old self-based existence, and into the new Spirit-energized life. All that remains is that we see who we have become, and make the decision to lift ourselves out of the well-worn tracks of the flesh.

Christ has no more that he can add to this scenario, his part is completed in every regard, the new heart is fully installed and ready to pump-out works of the Spirit. It is a perfectly functioning replica of his own heart, ready and waiting for us to abandon ourselves to its full potential – all that remains is that we change our minds and let go.

To change our minds requires the biggest leap ever contemplated by humanity – it is a change that is so dramatic that we cease to be the person we were. We choose to become a person who abandons the way of living that has served us for our whole life. This old way of living will continue to function as it always has if that is our choice, our flesh screams out "if it ain't broke don't fix it" – but our spirit glimpses the invisible possibilities… *will we let go?*

Chapter 11.
Letting Go.

RELINQUISHING control is not the sort of thing we do easily. It defies our in-built responses to lift our hands off the steering wheel and let the vehicle go where it likes. It is a self-preservation instinct to hold on to control of a car – *and the same is true regarding the way we live our lives.*

We would not normally relinquish control without a good reason. We would not normally relinquish control without some sort of emergency or other extraordinary situation – unfortunately the flesh has convinced us that no such emergency exists, *everything is as it should be.*

But that is not the case. An extraordinary situation is very much before us – we are attempting to navigate our way through the rapids of life in an old worn-out canoe that Christ retired 2000 years ago.

Religion has talked-up the seaworthiness of this old jalopy; it has convinced us that this leaking vessel has the capacity to bring us home just as it always has. It has cautioned us about the merits of making a change mid-stream, and convinced us that it is better to be safe than sorry, and to stick with what you know.

But, religion doesn't know how to trust Jesus,
it doesn't know how to stake its life on the promises he makes.

Religion and the flesh are bed-fellows, they always go around together. Religion presents its counsel 'be cautious', and the flesh adds a resounding affirmation. They hold us back because they cannot see the potential that life holds, without the safety of 'holding on to control'.

The problem with holding on to control, is that we weren't design that way. We were designed to rest in the ability of God to hold us and keep us – it is how we were made back in the beginning.

We were designed to be carried aloft by the Spirit of God. Not in a physical flight, but a restful soaring upon the breath of God – we were designed to let go, and trust that he is better at living our lives than we are.

Does that sound a bit unreal? It might do – because we are by nature so unfamiliar with the concept.

I am not talking about some meditative state, or a yoga-like floating on some ethereal spiritual energy. I am talking about something far more tangible than that - I am talking about grasping once and for all that Jesus is everything he says he is, and casting our entire existence into his ability to hold us.

I am proposing that we were designed to be in union with God, and that God is the one who does all the 'doing' through us. Sure we still get up in the morning as usual, sure we still go about the usual activities of our day – but God bears the load, we determine to trust in his capacity / not our own, we determine to allow him to do what he always wanted – to fill us with his life.

This kind of restful union has been out of vogue in Christian circles for a long time. We have by-and-large opted for the *'don't be too presumptuous'* approach – and this safe ground has left us with such a meager spiritual life that we are hardly distinguishable from the unsaved.

It is a travesty; a complete disregard for the potency of the blood of Christ - that we could be so completely re-born with the very heart and nature of

God, and yet live our lives as if it was little more than a pleasant fairy tale we share.

The blood of Christ was shed that we might completely abandon ourselves to its amazing capacity to bear us through every moment of our lives. It was shed for so much more than the establishment of the institution we call the church – it was shed that we might live today and every day hidden with Christ in God – not doubting our standing with God, but casting ourselves head-long into his ability to present us to the Father, free from any stain or blemish.

This is letting go.

A word of caution: first make an examination of the work of Christ, learn to fix your eyes on him, become convinced that he can be trusted – *and then let go.*

There is no risk involved in this leap; it is not a leap into the dark. This 'letting go' can only be done when you finally realize that it would be a risk to retain control. The price of retaining control has become too great for you – because you would be walking away from the adventure you were made for, and settling for mere relative safety.

For those of us who have been around Christian circles for a long time; we have heard the sermons, shared in the small group discussions, and repeated all the well-worn Christians phrases… and then a cross road comes, it dawns on us that we have been speculating about God / but not actually trusting him as if he is God – we have been engaged in all the spiritual talk / but not actually casting our life into the certainty of it – *and we see ourselves as we really are, creatures of the culture.*

When that day comes it's time to let go.

It's important to understand that this 'letting go' is not some emotional response or action arising from religious fervor - it is the most reasonable response to make when faced with the love and kindness of God. It is not *yet another religious act,* which God requires of us so we can re-dedicate ourselves to his cause – quite the contrary; it is an action that has ourselves as the primary beneficiary. We cast our whole lives into Christ because it would defy reason not to. To hold back from entrusting Jesus with our entire being would be the height of foolishness.

It is surrendering of the very best kind, simply because he is much better at providing us with the best possible life than we are. We let him into everything, every dark corner and hidden thought, every relationship, ambition and pain – because he can truly be trusted to make everything beautiful – *if we will just let go.*

There is a view widely held among Christians that God has a plan, that his perfect will is to enlist us in that plan – and that once enlisted we lose our grip on the things we really want. This view causes many folk to act out a form of Christianity which is not surrendered at all. Sure they may engage in all of the activities on offer, but that is not the same as entrusting our entire existence into his love.

In reality, God's plan is that we be found 'in Christ', surrendered to his love.

Any service or action we might engage in, over-and-above that surrender, is irrelevant - *if we have not first grasped the magnitude of his love for us and cast every fiber of our being into its safety.*

Chapter 12.
Life On The Other Side.

John 5:24 speaks of the fact that we <u>have already</u> crossed over from death to life. It is a past tense event that took place when we received Jesus as our savior. We don't see the full reality of this status until we close our eyes in death. But then we shall see with clarity… *that which has been ours all along.*

Ephesians 2:19 and Philippians 3:20 speak of our citizenship in heaven; it is a present tense citizenship that we have now, we don't have to wait till we die to get it. This citizenship became ours as part of the package deal when we became a believer – there is no Christian who has ever walked on the face of the earth that was not a fully-fledged citizen of heaven. Our citizenship is not subject to the vagaries of our Christian walk in the same way church membership is, we cannot be excommunicated because of bad behavior. Our behavior was irrelevant in the initial transaction and it is irrelevant in keeping it, we are citizens of heaven because Christ purchased our membership, and gave it to us for free.

Knowing that we have 'crossed over from death to life' and that we are fully paid up 'citizens of heaven', you would think that every believer would entrust every aspect of their existence to Jesus – it seems the most logical, reasonable, thing to do.

To a large extent this isn't the case - because our identity is so wrapped up in navigating our way through 'good and evil' on planet earth, that we can't imagine a life where we relinquish control and hand the navigation role to Jesus. We can't imagine that God can take the mess we call 'our life' and do any better with the whole 'good and evil thing' than we are.

The lie 'that the flesh counts' has kept us focused on the issues of life for so long, that we can't visualize an alternative. We may have asked God to help from time to time, we may have prayed, and even begged for his help – but that is not the way God planned it to work. His plan is to live within us permanently, not to give us a touch of his life from time to time, *as the need arises.*

God doesn't respond to our desperation, he doesn't respond to our sincerity or passion – he responds to Christ in us, and our only part is to lose ourselves into the loving goodness of Jesus by deeply trusting him, and letting go of all reservation.

It takes great courage to approach the throne of God clothed only in the righteousness of Christ, all of our instincts tell us to bring some personal quality or religious activity. But when we shed all of the garments of the flesh, God sees only 'Christ in me' and I am welcomed just as he welcomes Jesus himself.

We cannot approach God partly dressed in the virtue of Christ and partly dressed in our own goodness. It is one or the other. Even if we feel we are mostly clothed in Christ's righteousness, and just wearing a small item of our own making, we might as well be entirely clothed in the filthy rags of fallen humanity – it is essential that we grasp the scale of the work that Christ did, and determine that it was more than enough to cover us.

There is often a contradiction between our confession / and the reality of our lives. We confess that Christ's righteousness is enough, but then we live lives insecure in the Fathers love – it is this contradiction that determines whether we are living as citizens of heaven, or attempting to hold dual citizenship.

As I have said earlier 'we are citizens of heaven', yet not all believers live in the place of their citizenship, choosing rather to hold a second citizenship in a foreign country that better suits their persuasions. If we are persuaded that 'the flesh counts' then we are living in a foreign land… *when our real home awaits our arrival and habitation.*

The intention of the gospel of Jesus is that people would relocate their existence into a new kingdom. We continue to live physically on the earth, but our real home is not here, it is in Christ. In that regard, Jesus did not come to be our example, the cause we follow, or even the purpose around which our life is focused – he came to kill all of the needy, instinctive responses of the flesh, and take us home early. Then indeed; the kingdom of God is within us.

Living in the Kingdom of God is a completely different ball game than our previous life – everything operates differently, none of the old ways apply.

Our tendency is to simply overlay the modus-operandi of this earthly realm onto the kingdom of God. We assume that they work in much the same way, except that the kingdom of God is a better, happier place.

In reality they bear little resemblance at all.

The motivations, purposes and values of our old place of citizenship are the result of Adam's choice to set up his own system – they are as different to the kingdom of God as night and day. We expect that the currency of the old kingdom continues to have buying power in the new kingdom, that our sense of identity and self-worth continues to be derived from our lifestyle choices, and adherence to a good code of living.

But there is an altogether different currency in the kingdom of God – *the blood of Christ.*

Sure we continue to live decent, well behaved lives (why wouldn't we) – but this behavior has no buying power what-so-ever in God's economy. Only faith in the life, death and resurrection of Jesus has any trading power in the kingdom of God. Even the most virtuous, charitable life holds no more value than filthy rags, *if we do it to position ourselves for God's favor.*

You might be thinking "can't I do both – can't I live a life of good deeds, as well as trust in Jesus"? Of course we can do both, in fact we should do both – but what we must not do is present our good deeds to God to attract his presence, favor or blessing. These are ours because Christ relocated us into God's kingdom – period!

It is this defining aspect of the kingdom of God that we must bring into our daily lives on the earth. God does not perceive us apart from our union with Christ, and neither does he perceive us apart from our citizenship in heaven. As far as he is concerned, there is no individuality.

He is not looking over the banisters of heaven down on to the earthly realm, and smiling his approval as we make our pilgrimage through life – he relates to us as those living within his kingdom in perfect union with his Son. We are permanent residents of his own kingdom – why would he relate to us as if we were stilled based in the very kingdom that he saved us from!

Think about someone who has left this earthly life in death, and gone to glory. Do you picture them going cap in hand to the Father for a hand-out of his blessing? Do you perceive them tip-toeing around the corridors of heaven, as if they are there by mistake? Do you imagine them bowing and scraping to every angelic being they happen to encounter? Of course not, the bible clearly declares that we are joint heirs with Christ, that we are seated with him in heavenly places, and that we will even judge the angels.

> *Surely if we have already crossed over from death to life,*
> *then we should be living right now*
> *as people who are completely at home in God's kingdom and presence.*

God has far less trouble than we do with the notion that we are favored guests around the banquet of his love and goodness – isn't it time we started to agree with God, instead of the debilitating lie satan gave us!

Do we really believe that God wants us to be timid in his presence, or doubting our place in his kingdom – he sent Jesus to resolve that once and for all,

Chapter 12. Life On The Other Side.

he wants us to grasp our salvation with both hands and revel in it with boldness and confidence. He wants us to value the sacrifice of his Son so highly that we embrace his salvation with complete abandon – giving no further thought for our weak human condition, but losing ourselves into our new re-born union with Jesus.

This is the best possible way we can express our thanks to Jesus – not by a life of servitude, and an attitude of unworthiness, but by a life that values the blood of Christ so highly that not one drop is wasted on the false humility of the flesh.

We are a new breed, we have the heart of Christ himself – dare we begin to actually live that way.

Chapter 13.
How Big Is Our Salvation?

I read an article some time ago which argued that Christians should be careful not to be too presumptuous of God – it seemed to be aimed at the excesses of some groups who advocate a posture of boldly demanding their inheritance from God, some have labeled these Christians 'the name it, and claim it crowd'. This article suggested that God values our humility and circumspection, and that such qualities are the correct posture for a mature Christian.

It reminded me of a prayer we used to say when I was a kid; "Gentle Jesus meek and mild, look upon a little child, Pity my simplicity, suffer me to come to thee"… *some things seems to have a way of sticking with you for life.*

It seems to me that we Christians are more likely to underestimate the scale of our salvation, than overestimate it. We are more likely to err on the side of caution - and put Jesus in the 'meek and mild' box, and ourselves in the 'pitifully simple' box. We consider it dangerous and ungodly to raise our expectations too high or perceive ourselves too loftily, in the fear that we might offend God with our brash behavior.

Such a point of view has its origins in the lie we inherited from Adam, it assumes that God values pleasing human behavior (especially of the humble kind), above the courageous faith that stands boldly upon the work of Christ. Ultimately this pleasing human behavior is elevated above the blood of Christ, with the result that the flesh has been given the credit once more.

The Lie We Like Best

This is not a discussion about whether Christians should behave with kindness and consideration (that is a given), but rather that these characteristics have become the hallmarks of Christianity, when we should be identified by our unyielding confidence in the blood of Christ. We have become a community of Ned Flanders, when we were redeemed for much more than such sticky sweetness.

John the Baptist was known for his fiery tongue, he called the Pharisees a 'brood of vipers' and demanded that they 'produce fruit fit for repentance' – yet in Matthew 11:11 Jesus says "Truly I tell you, among those born of women there has not risen anyone greater than John the Baptist; yet whoever is least in the kingdom of heaven is greater than he".

We are in the kingdom of heaven (meaning that we are born of God), John the Baptist was too. In the context of his earthly origins he was the greatest of all - yet Jesus says that we are greater than John was, because of our divine re-birth. It is this exceptional aspect of our new nature that propels us into a godly boldness, it is the opposite to the ambitions of the flesh – because it is nothing without Christ / yet everything with him.

Our self-talk is generally reflective of how we view ourselves. Such statements as 'I'm hopeless' or 'I will never amount to much' are evidence of a troubled inner condition. The world has developed a remedy for poor self-talk, it has come up with a range of positive mantras to counter our weak inner condition 'just do it', 'be your best', to name a few. Christianity has also jumped on the self-talk bandwagon, with statements like 'you are a champion' or 'be the hero inside you' heard regularly from the Sunday gurus.

This pumped-up self-talk is not the renewed mind that we read about in Romans 12:2. We don't renew our mind by changing the language that we speak out, we renew our mind by grasping that Jesus has made his home in us – and his presence transforms us from the inside out, in a way that positive self-talk can't (because it attempts to work from the outside in).

In a nut shell, we can live great lives - because we are great… not vise-versa.

Chapter 13. How Big Is Our Salvation?

There is no showiness in this, no self-promotion – simply an acknowledgement that Christ completed the most remarkable transformation possible. He took the worst of self-righteous sinners, and made us into the divinely-righteous ones. He took the losers of the world and filled them with himself, so they became the greatest beings to ever walk the planet – this is the scale of the salvation from which our boldness is derived.

The importance of understanding the scale of our salvation cannot be overstated, it is the difference between a life of mediocre flesh-manufactured righteousness, and to walk on the earth as a man or woman transformed into the substance of Christ. Not merely a man or woman who is representing Christ, but one who is actually made of Christ.

I know that many will find this sort of talk excessive or even repulsive, that it smacks of self-promotion – yet it really is the essence of the gospel. Paul himself said "I no longer live, but Christ lives in me" - this wasn't because Paul had finally crucified the flesh, and Christ was now able to inhabit his soul – it was because Christ had crucified Paul's flesh for him, and Paul simply leaned back into Christ for his new identity.

The prayer I prayed as a kid was wrong *(sorry Mum)*, I didn't need to ask Christ to 'suffer me to come to him', Christ had already made his home in me, *and we couldn't get any closer than that.* This little prayer epitomized the thinking of the church I grew up in… we should have been taught to thank Jesus that we had come to him already, on a lonely hill outside Jerusalem 2000 years ago, we should have been taught to value his daily presence in us, that cost him his very life. Instead we doubted his work because the weaknesses of the flesh became the measure of the work of Christ.

Similarly during Holy Communion we would recite a declaration that we were "poor miserable sinners". The fact is; we had our sinfulness nailed to the cross once and for all when Jesus died. Our sinful condition is past tense – yet every time we approached the communion table we declared that Christ's salvation was small, that it had only dealt with our sinfulness for a month or so, and then we needed to confess our sinfulness all over again – *(now that is what I call bad self-talk!)*

Perhaps a humble confession of our weak nature is acceptable before we receive salvation, and to acknowledge our human condition would not be out of line before Christ's transformation has been wrought in us - but it is offensive to talk in that way after we have been joined to Christ. Such talk belittles a salvation that is immeasurably greater than we could ever think or imagine, and it undermines the life of faith that Christ died to give us.

Our salvation is not theoretical or positional; it is a fact - as real now as it will be when we pass from this earthly life. And it is as complete while we go around in our earth suits, as it will be when we shed them and at last see ourselves for what we were all along – *(but for the veil of our natural sight).*

Once again let me say, this is not simply a matter of changing our language into a more positive confession, or stopping ourselves from thinking negative thoughts – it requires a pilgrimage to the cross. We return again and again and view the cross of Christ, asking God what it was all about – until finally the magnitude of that event breaks through, and we see that Jesus completed the impossible – *he made me as perfect as God.*

Chapter 14.
Seated In Heavenly Places.

The scripture in Ephesians 2:6 has quoined an unusual turn of phrase, "And God raised us up with Christ and seated us with him in the heavenly realms in Christ Jesus". It sounds to me as though Paul finds the language available to human beings lacking in its ability to describe this new location.

Heavenly realms, heavenly places – *up there somewhere!*

But Paul clarifies the full meaning of this location by adding the words "in Christ Jesus".

It took the better part of my life to dial-down the lie that 'Christianity was all about my good living', so that I could finally hear the real message – that the point of my Christianity was that I be found 'in Christ Jesus'.

Being 'in Christ Jesus' is a little hard to get our heads around at first. We are wired up to understand geography from a purely physical perspective. We often try to locate heaven, or hell, or even God geographically, but we need to remember that these locations are in a realm that bears no resemblance to our natural realm – in fact the natural realm is a mere shadow of something that is vastly greater, yet not viewed by the natural eye.

The constraints of distance, time and knowledge are unique to the natural environment – the eternal realm has no such limitations, and such statements as "Christ is all, and is in all" (Colossians 3:11) is completely at home there.

As I started to open my eyes to the real message of Christianity I began to see many references to 'Christ in me' and 'in Christ Jesus' repeated throughout the New Testament. It seemed as though my focus on the work of the flesh, had filtered out the gospel message that was before me the whole time.

> *The term 'in Christ' is repeated so consistently*
> *through the letters of the apostles,*
> *that I now view my salvation as being entirely defined by that one thing.*

I am not a Christian because I go to church, am involved in various types of service, worship, pray, or read the word – I am a Christian because Christ has crucified my dead spirit and replaced it with his own perfect Spirit. Though I may participate in many activities in response to this defining fact, these activities do not make me / or add to, my status 'in Christ'.

Now that I have made this shift in my thinking, I am able to take it a step further and see that wherever Christ is *in the spiritual realm* – I am there also. In fact; there is nowhere that Christ goes, where I do not also go.

We know that Christ is seated at the right hand of the Father from Mark 6:19 – accordingly my position as 'seated in heavenly places' is the logical progression. Wherever Christ is – there am I, wherever I am - there is Christ.

He is not my alter-ego or my conscience, he is not my moral compass or my life coach – he is my actual identity. Sure I retain my unique personality, appearance and intellect – these are the unique characteristics of my soul, but the real me (my spirit) has been possessed by Jesus so profoundly, that the Father doesn't even look twice when I enter the throne room of heaven.

It is this spiritual status that enables scriptures like Hebrews 10:19-22 to make sense; "we have confidence to enter the Most Holy Place by the blood of Jesus".

I do not enter the presence of God when I pray or worship, I am always in the presence of God by virtue of my union with Christ (who is in union with the Father) – and now by faith I partake of that presence, simply by believing it to be true.

This believing is different to the believing I used to have.

I used to believe in a way that engaged my intellect, and to an extent my lifestyle also – it was a believing that had grey areas, things I couldn't be absolutely sure of – so my life didn't really change much as a result. This believing was more based on hope and speculation than certainty; *it was the best my natural understanding could produce.* It resulted in more of a culturally-based Christianity, than an unshakable faith – you could say that I had one foot in each camp, (confidence/speculation).

But my new believing goes way beyond that; it involved the 'crossing of a line' – I had to determine what was true and cast myself unreservedly into that truth. At first the only truth I was prepared to hang my hat on, was that Jesus had died for my sins – so I crossed that line, and determined that it was a fact that I would never revisit again. I burned that bridge behind me, and cast myself entirely into it as a 'not-negotiable fact'.

It wasn't so much that I previously doubted the fact of Christ's death for my sins, but rather that the lie I harbored within me, kept me from giving myself completely and boldly to the truth of it. The lie that 'the flesh counts' had me examining my response and lifestyle as the triggers for the operation of Christ's presence in my life, rather than examining the substance of Christ's work itself. I could not abandon myself to the integrity of Christ's work because I was too aware of my inadequate response to it.

> ***The log-jamb was only resolved when I ran out of self-based responses, and simply decided to believe.***

Up until then I didn't realize there was anything lacking in my believing. I was believing in the same way that everyone else did, the whole culture operated this way – we were big on the rhetoric of Christianity, but small on the bridge-burning confidence. At best, we thought God would come through if we operated within the principles outlined in his word, but it was always future tense and hinged on our satisfaction of godly principles. I know now that principles, confessions, and spiritual activities do not engage the presence of God in our lives – he became re-engaged 2000 years ago, and we partake in this engagement now *by believing it*.

I have introduced the matter of believing at this point because it is integral to our participation in the outcomes of Christ's death and resurrection.

Even though all of the truth contained in the word of God is the inheritance of every believer on the planet, it does not become the reality of our daily lives unless we believe it.

> *God doesn't force the wonders of our salvation upon us;*
> *he simply shows us the truth and invites us to join-in by believing it.*

He destroyed the work of the enemy over our lives, he re-made us into a new race of divine-natured beings – and then he invited us to walk away from the legacy of Adam, and the lie it wrote on our hearts, and believe a new thing "the Spirit gives life".

Here lies the battle ground for Christians, it is here that our victory on this earth is won or lost. We do not need to engage with satan, he was crushed by the work of Christ; he has no power over us. But we do need to send his lie back to hell where it came from. He will continue to maintain the lie if we allow him, with the result that we will live a form of Christianity that is half-formed at best.

If we 'burn the bridge' to his lie and cast ourselves fully into the truth which is 'Christ and Him crucified', then our salvation can expand to full maturity – the choice is ours, to believe a lie / or not.

Chapter 15.
Disposing Of The Lie.

THE first thing that is necessary in disposing of the debilitating lie that we inherited from Adam, is to acknowledge its existence.

It is a lie that is buried deep down, and it has no intention of rising to the surface so we can have a good look at it – all we can do is look at the trail of destruction that it has left upon the history of humanity, as evidence of its existence.

The second thing to do is to accept that 'the lie' is not supposed to be there.

The second thing is probably the hardest.

It's hardest because we don't instinctively know how to walk as Adam did at the very start. Our flesh has concealed our original design so well, that we have no capacity to grasp a way of living that does not depend on 'the lie'. Our mental faculties simply don't understand the statement 'Christ in me', we always reduce it to a figurative, or positional reality, rather than the actual truth of our existence.

The reason this happens is that we continue to apply the 'receivers' of the flesh as we attempt to understand the workings of the Spirit. Our five senses and our intellect (our earthly receivers) do a great job of relating to physical information, but they have no capacity to accurately discern matters of the spiritual realm. We can only grasp spiritual truth when we shut down our natural 'receivers', and re-open the 'eyes of the heart'.

Our true identity is the Spirit within us, the realm in which it exists cannot be perceived by the 'receivers' of the flesh.

Our five senses and our intellect can only interpret truth based on the physical realities that they observe. They see our imperfect lifestyles and frequent failings (they reason that God's word can only be interpreted through the filter of these weaknesses) - with the result that the truth is diluted to agree with the reasonings of the flesh.

The eyes of our heart on the other hand, do not observe the imperfections of humanity; all they can see is the stunning accomplishments of the blood of Christ. So crystal-clear is their view of the scale of the work of Christ, that the weaknesses of the flesh are seen for what they really are from God's perspective - nothing more than the lingering foolish lives of people who haven't grasped the scale of Christ's work in them.

Our natural receivers observe the good deeds of humankind, they take-in the vast landscape of religious activity, fellowship, and service, and they get so caught-up in the excitement and fervor of the human response to God – that Christ is seen as little more than the model upon which the human response was built.

Our spiritual receivers observe a completely different landscape. The response of humanity is so meager in comparison with the accomplishments of Christ, that it doesn't even warrant acknowledgement. The 'eyes of the heart' see a view of Christ that is so much more than just a man who 'did and said' some great things when he was on the earth - they see the most lavish love, the most creative life, and the most shining glory in the realm of the Spirit – and they see this splendor overwhelming us as the objects of its focus.

This overwhelming splendor completely eclipses the endeavors of humanity to the point of irrelevance. It is not that human endeavors are not of note; it's just that they don't rate when compared to the surpassing greatness of Christ.

In other words, the issue is not whether we should acknowledge some relative value in the works that are produced by the flesh, but that these works have

Chapter 15. Disposing Of The Lie.

distracted us from something which is so spectacular by comparison, that they are rendered as worth no more than junk.

When this in understood then the 'lie' is disenfranchised, we have denied the 'lie' its vote in our lives.

The lie that 'the flesh counts' attempts to elevate the works of the flesh to equality with the works of Christ. It does this; not only by magnifying the flesh, but more especially, by diminishing the work of Christ. Accordingly, the work of Christ is understood through our natural receivers as - a good example, a life of suffering, a martyr's death. These are the observations made in the physical realm, but they barely scratch the surface in fully revealing what Christ did.

These naturally observed facts could also be applied to any man or woman who has lived a selfless life; Gandhi, Mandela, Mother Theresa – in fact, many churches teach that Christ was an example of *'a life of value'* in much the same vein as these highly regarded people.

The flesh measures value based on visibly observable virtues.

The spirit measures value on so much more than the visible evidence, it goes beyond the accumulated sins of humanity (for which Christ suffered the punishment), and observes a spiritual event that is so astounding by comparison, that the visible event pales into the background.

This 'behind the scenes' event is the one that truly matters, because it sets us free from the lie.

While Christ was suffering the punishment for our sins on the hill outside Jerusalem, he was also engaged in the most profound transformation imaginable. The divine nature (which was the essence of his being), was hauled out of him – and in its place he was injected with the godless, sin filled nature of humanity.

He became sin.

For the second time in history the saddest of all laments rang out – "*My God, my God, why have you forsaken me?*"

It was the only way that we could be returned to our union with God.

> ***We had to get a divine nature from somewhere***
> ***(God couldn't fellowship with sin)***
> ***– and so Jesus put his hand up, and said "I will give them mine".***

The second Adam (Jesus) did a hostage exchange with the devil. He said to satan, "I will become the first Adam (and all his seed that followed), those you have had in chains for the millennia". I will allow myself to be transformed into the sick experiment of humanity; its sinful, wicked, and self-based nature will become my nature – and in its place, they will be given back my nature, the nature they started with.

Satan agreed.

And so Jesus completed a 'behind the scenes' exchange that beggars belief; he became the godless, fallen nature of humanity – so that we could become the perfect, divine nature of God.

"My God, my God, why have you forsaken me?"

This lament is the cry of the God-forsaken. God did more than turn his face away from the load of sin that was placed on to Jesus; he locked Jesus out of the Garden which was his true home, and so he wandered in the hopeless netherworld of sin and death, the home of all who bear the fallen nature of Adam.

You may be thinking, "This is tragic beyond belief".

This is the stuff of such sadness and grief that was seen by the prophet Isaiah when he wrote "Surely he took up our pain and bore our suffering, yet we considered him punished by God, stricken by him, and afflicted".

Chapter 15. Disposing Of The Lie.

The word 'stricken' means; "Struck or wounded, overwhelmed by disease, trouble, or painful emotion, to be incapacitated or disabled".

This is the package deal that came upon Christ with our fallen nature.

This tragedy takes on even greater proportions when you consider that the people, for whom this terrible event was suffered, make such a meager connection with it. Perhaps it is too shocking to contemplate, so we choose to remain within the safe boundaries of the observations of the flesh. Whatever the reason - once seen for what it truly is, this revelation changes everything.

It exposes the lie once and for all
– our attachment to the ambitions of the flesh is intolerable,
when we see at last the scale of the thing that Christ did.

As always the flesh is quick to respond "what must I do?" And now at last the spirit can reply with confidence "you can do nothing, Christ has done it all". You can do nothing because you were crucified with Christ, there is no you – there is only Christ. Turn away from the security you have built-up around yourself through your self-made life, and lean into Christ for everything.

Song of Songs 8:5 "Who is this coming up from the desert 'leaning' on her lover?"

It is us - he paid such a price that we might lean into him.

Chapter 16.
Indestructible Life.

THE ambitions of satan take an interesting turn in Hebrews 7:16 "one who has become a priest not on the basis of a regulation as to his ancestry, but on the basis of *the power of an indestructible life*".

Jesus could let go.

He let the fallen nature of humanity overtake his being – because he knew something that satan didn't know. He leaned into his Fathers love because he knew that the 'indestructible life' of God was greater than the power of satan, sin and death.

So he simply leaned into the security of his Father's love - and allowed the whole terrible thing to crush him.

Why?

Hebrews 12:2 "Let us fix our eyes on Jesus, the pioneer and perfecter of our faith, who *for the joy set before Him* endured the cross, scorning its shame, and sat down at the right hand of the throne of God".

Because he knew his Father is why!

He knew his Fathers plan would succeed, and that he and the human race had a joy that lay before them – a joy that could not be thwarted by satan's manipulations of the flesh. Jesus had no doubt about the ultimate outcome of this terrible journey he had to take, he never thought for a moment that he would be lost forever in the collective sinfulness of the human race. Terrible as this journey would be, Jesus always knew that the foolish experiment of humanity would be no match for the indestructible life of God.

We find accounts of Jesus crucifixion in all of the gospels. In both Matthew and Mark we read his morbid cry "My God, My God, why have you forsaken me?" And in the gospel of Luke we also read words that are not as clearly stated in the others. Luke 23:46, Jesus called out with a load voice, "Father, into your hands I commit my spirit".

Even though Jesus sensed that he had been 'forsaken' by his Father - he still committed his Spirit to him as he gave up his life!

He knew something about his Father that has been hidden from our sight by the lie. He knew that the self-righteous independence of fallen humanity would report to him that the Father had turned his face away, and he also knew in his heart that God will never abandon the human spirit which was the un-witting casualty of satan's deception.

God wouldn't abandon the rebellious human race, and he wouldn't abandon the Lamb of God that was sacrificed in their place. So Jesus simply let go, and committed his Spirit to that knowledge.

The lie has within it the ability to shut-out the knowledge of God that is so necessary for us to 'let go' as Jesus did. The flesh has pulled the blind down over the true knowledge of God (it has re-made him in its own image). Jesus had no such problem, he knew his Father – he knew that although he was about to enter a state of independence from God, that this did not imply a similar response from his Father.

The flesh nature would cause him to lose sight of his Father, but his Father's love would remain intact – *(in spite of the inability of his flesh to see it)*. Jesus would lose the operation of 'the eyes of his heart' – but he knew he was safe in his Father, in spite of what his senses told him.

The flesh hides the truth.

The flesh reports information which debilitates humanity – "God has forsaken us".

But God cannot forsake humanity, we are his offspring. The fact remains however; Adams choice to clothe humanity in the flesh has obscured the Heart of God from us. Like Adam did before us, we fear God and hide from him. Jesus came to return to us the spiritual sight that humanity started with - so that we will let go and commit our spirits to that amazing knowledge of him again. This is the opposite of fearing and hiding, it is more akin to confidently leaning-in to his love.

We read in 2 Timothy 2:13 "if we are faithless, he will remain faithful for he cannot disown himself" – the faithless choices and lifestyle of humanity have not caused God to change toward us, however they have caused us to lose the ability to see his faithfulness toward us.

> *Even after Jesus lost sight of his Father,*
> *he continued to lean-in to the Fathers love.*

Imagine the 'prodigal son' – he takes the journey of the flesh and leaves behind his father's love. As his life deteriorates he remembers his father, but the wanton life he has led convinces him that the father would not want him back as a son – *just a servant*. It was his choice to walk away from his father and enter a self-absorbed lifestyle that obscures his father's heart from him – however this perspective was proven wrong, his father was longing for his return the whole time he was away.

We have had this spiritual sight returned to us; we can see the Father's heart as it really is. The eyes of our heart can see again *(though they may not see too well for lack of use)* - our part is to return to the modus-operandi that Jesus used, and commit our spirit to God's love just as he did, in spite of the circumstances that may confront us and convince us that we are beyond the reach of God's love.

To lose sight of God is a terrifying thing - it is the very thing that the lie was sent by satan to do, and for thousands of years it achieved its goal. But now we can see him again, and the image of him becomes clearer and clearer as we learn to fix our eyes on Jesus. We lift our eyes off the failings of the flesh, and on to the competence of Christ.

In Genesis 3:7 we read "Then the eyes of both of them were opened, and they realized they were naked" – the eyes of the flesh came into operation and reported their unrighteousness to them. These were not their physical eyes (Eve could already see the fruit and its pleasing appearance in verse 6) – but their act of independence revealed their spiritual depravity, as the eyes of the flesh began to operate.

Unfortunately, the eyes of the flesh – and the eyes of the heart (see Ephesians 1:18), cannot operate together, we cannot alternate between the two. Jesus came to give us back the spiritual sight which belongs to the divine nature – we must choose to use it, and shut down the sight of the flesh.

Let me say it again; the fears that we carry through life are the result of a lack of spiritual sight. If we could see that the Heavenly Father is fully engaged with us then we would heave a massive sigh of relief and relax, we would commit ourselves into his love and lean fully in to his ability to carry us through. But we don't because our flesh continues to report that God has forsaken us - *in response to our inadequate lives.*

Jesus reconnected us into the Father through himself; <u>our part is to see it.</u>

To see God is an extraordinary thing, anything is possible, everything is ours.

Jesus walked on planet earth for his whole life with a clear view of the Father; it enabled him to do extraordinary things. It was only when Jesus was afflicted with the fallen nature of humanity that he groped around to see his Father. In the very same instant that Jesus cried out "Where are you Father?" the eyes of humanity were opened to see him. Jesus lost sight of his Father, so that we could see him – *the exchange was completed.*

Now we walk planet earth as Jesus did, he humbled himself and became like humanity (just like you and me) – *but for the fallen nature.* Philippians 2:7 tells us; "who, though he was in the form of God, did not count equality with God a thing to be grasped". It was Jesus divine nature that gave him spiritual sight *(in the form of God)* - in every other regard he emptied himself, to be no more than we are. And now we have the divine nature that he had, and our spiritual sight has been restored – it becomes clearer day-by-day as we reject the lie, and begin to believe that the work of Christ has transformed us back into his image.

The estrangement between the Father and the flesh is real, light cannot fellowship with darkness. Like the prodigal son, we can easily assign this estrangement to the Father's judgmental attitude of our inability to measure-up to his standards. But when we do that, we engage the lie of satan as our means of understanding the Father's heart – this is where we go wrong.

This estrangement is our choice not the Father's (the prodigal son walked away) – the re-engagement is the Father's initiative, he sent Jesus to bring us home. His heart was yearning for reunion all along, and he made it happen in spite of us, because he cannot deny his love for us.

Chapter 17.
The Father's Heart.

THE flesh is convinced that everything happens in response or reaction, to itself.

The flesh thinks it is the center of the universe and every occurrence is in some way connected to it, and its activities.

Over the years (since Adam and Eve made their exit from the presence of God), the flesh has built up a view of life through experience and observation. It is a 'karma like' point of view, which has determined that everything that takes place in life is somehow related to what we do, and how we live. Much like Newton's third law "Every action, results in an equal and opposite reaction" – we see life as a complex arrangement of responses to our own actions.

The flesh has managed to overlay this principle onto the 'Heart of God'. We have bound him to the workings of the natural world, but he is way above nature and is bound by no such limitations.

God is motivated by his heart only.

Galatians 6:7 says; "Do not be deceived: God cannot be mocked. A man reaps what he sows." We are used to looking for a principle or formula as we read God's word – and this scripture seems to deliver one very neatly into our hands. But as we read further we find it is really all about the nature that we choose to base our lives on – God is not linking his response to our actions, but rather is providing us with an alternative to the 'cause and effect' life we were trapped in.

God is mocked when we attempt to gain the benefits of his kingdom, through the means of the flesh.

In other words; even though we have chosen a basis for our lives that has blocked his loving goodness being expressed, he has provided an alternative in spite of the rules that we set up – he provided a way back to his heart in spite of us.

He is above the rule of 'cause and effect'.

Romans 5:8 "But God demonstrates his own love for us in this: While we were still sinners, Christ died for us" – this is the way God's heart works, he doesn't wait for us to get our act together – he just provides our salvation because he can *(and because he cannot deny himself)*.

Satan thought he had God cornered, he thought God was bound by the legal process of 'retribution for sin' – but God's love was bigger, and he crafted a solution based on his heart, not the law *(even though it satisfied the law)*, he exchanged the life of Jesus - for the life of fallen humanity. God's love was never in question; the only issue was the cost to him that would be required to express that love – and he paid that cost, because his love will never be directed, constrained, or limited by the law.

> *Jesus didn't come to satisfy some legal process*
> *– he came to express the love of God.*

For God so loved the world…

These words are familiar to the Christian community, more than perhaps any other verse in the bible, yet we have lost much of the significance of them in the clutter of church life – God loves, because of who he is, not because of who we are.

And that is just the point; God does not love us (or hate us for that matter), because of who we are – he loves us because of who he is. That is the opposite of karma – that is the heart of God.

So we need to recalibrate our understanding of the heart of God without the influence of the flesh.

God is love!

Unlike us, God does not love human attributes, he loves human beings.

He loves because it is the stuff he is made of.

I'm not trying to be mushy here, this is not an emotional thing – God loves for reasons much higher than our emotions could ever reach, he loves because if he ceased to love, he would cease to be God. It is in him; he could no sooner 'cease to love' and remain God – as we could no sooner 'cease to breathe', and remain alive.

Yet there is a reason that goes even further beyond this, that is both magnificent and surprising. He loves us because we are a part of him. He loves himself in the purest way possible, and he is indeed worthy of that love because he is lovely in every regard. And he loves us because we are a part of his own lovely nature.

God loves himself? *He knows his worth.*

As I said earlier, God's love is not constrained within the workings of human emotions (or ego). He can love himself because he is the supreme origin of all goodness. There is no other source in existence which independently generates goodness – it all emanates from God.

The emotions of love that we feel on earth are a mere shadow of the love of God. We love because of earthly environmental reasons; our love is always from and towards the objects of creation *(we love God also but can find it difficult to locate him, and so we often opt to love Jesus as his representative in the natural realm).*

God's love is dramatically superior to this earthbound love – there is no factor or quality within the natural realm that attracts his love, even the best of humanity falls way short. He loves us because he made us in his own image.

In Mark 10:18 Jesus makes a surprising statement; "As Jesus started on His way, a man ran up and knelt before Him. Good Teacher, he asked, what must I do to inherit eternal life? Why do you call Me good? Jesus replied, No one is good except God alone."

Jesus appears to be denying that he is good, but in reality he is saying that God is the only source of real goodness – and without his union to the Father, he is no different to anyone else. That might sound odd - to suggest that Jesus wasn't inherently good in himself seems to be risky ground, but it's worth thinking about.

Don't get me wrong; I am not trying to make a case that Jesus was less than perfect - quite the contrary, I am suggesting that Jesus was absolutely perfect because he and the Father were one. It was the union that he had with his Father that established Jesus as a perfect man, and by confidently resting is his Fathers love he was as perfect as his Father. It wasn't until he bore upon himself the fallen nature of humankind, that his Fathers perfect nature was cut off from him – *but never his love.*

Jesus said these words in John 5:26 "For as the Father has life in himself, so he has granted the Son to have life in himself". Jesus is speaking here of spiritual life, or eternal life - it was a life that had the Father as its source. If the Father had not granted that Jesus would have this life, then Jesus would be spiritually dead – *the Father is the source of life.*

Chapter 17. The Father's Heart.

Again in John 6:57 Jesus says "Just as the living Father sent me and I live because of the Father, so the one who feeds on me will live because of me" Jesus lives (eternal life) because the <u>living</u> Father gives him life, he feeds on his Fathers love and it gives him life. And then he invites us to partake of himself, and live also.

The scriptures also tell us that God is love. We would normally interpret that to mean that God has pure love, the best kind of love, the divine kind of love – but what if it actually means that there is no love, but for the love that is God. He is the origin; love comes from no other place but God. Humanity has many forms of love, but they are not the same as God's love – my love may be deep, emotional and strong, but it is a mere shadow of the divine love that continually emanates from God. God is more than full of love – <u>He is love</u>.

In John 15:9 Jesus says "As the Father has loved me, so have I loved you. Now remain in my love" Jesus remained in his Fathers love, and it gave him life. When we remain-in (feed on) Jesus love, we have the same life that sustained Jesus.

What kind of love is this that produces spiritual life?

It is a selfless love that gives perfection to whomever desires. In John 16:15 Jesus says "All that belongs to the Father is mine", and in John 17:10 he says "(Father) All I have is yours, and all you have is mine". It is this selfless giving heart of God that enables Jesus to do everything that the Father asked of him. Jesus did not die for humanity because God commanded him to; rather it was a joyful privilege to fulfill his Fathers desire for humanity. Jesus could not hold himself back from the radiant love that filled him, as the eyes of his heart beheld the unsearchable love of his Father.

All that belongs to the Father, all that he has, his radiant love - energized Jesus to do the unthinkable.

The Old Testament temple sacrifices were a shadow of the reality in heaven; they were a poor copy of the sacrifice of Christ, and alluded to the truth which was to come. This shadow was draped over the weakness of the flesh as a representation of the real thing which would do everything that the temple sacrifices couldn't – bring reunion between God and humanity.

We know better than to assign any real value to the law and sacrifices, the book of Hebrews makes it very plain that the Old Covenant was faulty. The thing we find more difficult is grasping the scale of the heart of God that was behind the sacrifice of Christ – we have no faculty to grasp such a thing, and so we view the love of God as much like human love only bigger, better, deeper, and stronger.

In other words we humanize God so that we can process who he is, and how he operates.

Paul groped around for superlatives that would adequately describe God's love; unsearchable, incomparable, love that surpasses knowledge – the greater Paul's revelation became, the more he was lost for words to express it. Yet we modern Christians have positioned God neatly into our doctrinal boxes, and contained him within human-like phrases – but he is beyond anything we can conceptualize, we *limit the unlimited* when we try to fit God's love into our neat and tidy, earthly understanding.

I say this for a very important reason; the degree to which we assign to God *human-like* characteristics, is the degree to which we limit the flow of life from his heart to ours.

This unsearchable love carried Jesus through the most shocking circumstances imaginable, we also must grasp the scale, and type of love, which flows from the heart of God - so that we too can face with bare-faced confidence all that life throws at us.

Our old nature tells us that we get through the issues of life by dedicating ourselves to the rules and principles of Christianity, it is convinced that God responds to our best efforts, and that there are certain steps we must carry out, to have his help. This is the only option open to us if the eyes of our heart are not functioning – it is all we can see.

Chapter 17. The Father's Heart.

There is a better way.

When we see the incomparable scale and magnificence of the Fathers heart towards us, we can do as Jesus did, and cast ourselves into the safety of that love. When we are most confident in God's love - then he is most lavish in his help in our time of need. When we put our confidence in the flesh by frantically dedicating ourselves to rules and principles, then we block God's help - and are back in Adam's predicament.

The whole point of the gospel is that we might have life. This life is from the Father - through Jesus - to us. It has the heart of God as its origin; it does not depend on the response of man, Christ has already positioned us to receive this life – our only part is to turn away from the lie 'that the flesh has a role to play in releasing it'.

Chapter 18.
Life-Principles V. Surrender.

There is no doubt that the bible is full of principles for successful living. From the 'Sermon on the Mount' delivered by Jesus, to Paul's many exhortations to the churches about Christian behavior – the bible is loaded with instructions and principles for right living. Not to mention the Old Testament, that contains the Ten Commandments, the proverbs, and many other directions for life.

The Old Covenant that God gave to Israel (which contained the 10 commandments, and many other rules and laws) was superseded as the system upon which we base our lives, when Jesus fulfilled it and subsequently made it obsolete.

But how do we craft a responsible life now that the Old Covenant is gone?

Jesus introduced a New Covenant (see Hebrews chapter 8) – our problem is that we bring to this new covenant a 'wrong premise' as the lens through which we attempt to understand it. We take the fallen (law based) mind-set of the Old Covenant, as the means by which we try to grasp the magnificence of the New Covenant.

The result is that we exchange 'like for like' – instead of sacrifices, laws, and commandments / we insert principles, methods, and behavior. With the result that we take a system that was designed by the flesh, re-label it, and call it works of the spirit. It is effectively the same system, because it depends on the efforts of man for its operation.

There is an alternative which eludes the masses because it can seem reckless, and irresponsible – yet it is the most sublime and excellent way for us to live. This alternative has as its center-piece the scripture from John 6:63 'The Spirit gives life, the flesh counts for nothing' – it disregards the merits of the flesh, and swings its focus across to the Spirit.

The fallen nature is insecure without the companionship of good principles and lifestyle; it is uncomfortable coming to God without the covering of respectability and decent behavior. The fallen nature fears that a life not defined by these things will descend into anarchy, it would be as irresponsible as driving a car without insurance.

The fallen nature is so obsessed with 'getting it right', that it doesn't realize that Jesus paid the insurance for us, and that the Holy Spirit is revving the engine waiting for us to hop in.

The eyes of the flesh do a very good job at observing reality within the natural realm, and the mind of the flesh does a very good job at reasoning through these observations, and arriving at sensible actions and responses. The problem for Christians is that our natural eyes are not able to observe spiritual things, and if they are our only source of input then our view of reality is seriously skewed.

If this deficiency is at play when we read the scriptures, then we will end up thinking Christianity is all about applying godly principles and lifestyle, as the means for crafting a successful Christian life. We will observe the workings of the natural realm, and assume that it applies to the spiritual realm, because we have no alternative input.

The natural realm and the spiritual realm are polar opposites.

CHAPTER 18. LIFE-PRINCIPLES V. SURRENDER.

Not that God intended it to be that way; he intended that the observations of the natural realm would be filtered through the renewed mind, so that these two realms would be in perfect harmony and agreement. We know that satan hijacked the natural realm, and became the ruler of this world – it is now impossible to see the reality of the spiritual realm, without the use of the eyes of our heart.

We are no longer citizens of the natural realm, our home is heaven, and we are aliens and strangers in the natural realm – our part is to begin seeing with our spiritual eyes so that we can live our lives from our new reality 'Christ in me'.

This present tense spiritual sight enables us to read the word of God afresh, and discover a more excellent way than the old system of principles and lifestyle.

The New Nature has a premise written into it which is opposed to the lie written onto the old nature. The Old Nature looked for the role of the flesh to define its identity; the New Nature has shifted its gaze away from the flesh and on to the stunning accomplishments of Christ. The Old Nature has no ability to view Christ, and so it will always seek out the role of the flesh.

The New Nature gets it – *'the Spirit gives life'* – so it looks to Christ only.

The Old Nature's inability to see the 'wonder of our union with Christ' renders it incapable of surrendering to his love and acceptance. In place of this letting go *(surrendering)*, it has fabricated a flesh-based counterfeit – it surrenders itself as a submissive slave, and gives the flesh an even greater role to play.

> *We were not redeemed for servitude; we were redeemed for son-ship.*

As we step into this son-ship, the Spirit of Christ within does indeed produce great acts of service, but we are never defined by what we do, only by the one with who we are in union. Works of life overflow from us like a fountain springing-up from Christ within, but these works (as valuable as they are) pale as we behold the glory of Christ and his great love for humanity.

So what of the many biblical exhortations to live right?

For those who no longer need to 'live right' to gain access to the favor of God, a new reason must be provided to justify the bible's apparent expectations of us. Galatians 5:25 provides that reason "Since we live by the Spirit, let us keep in step with the Spirit". This verse tells Christians to be true to themselves – they are already spiritually alive, so it makes sense to bring our natural lives into agreement with the spiritual reality.

In the preceding verses (16 to 24), Paul describes the difference between living according to the Old Nature and the New Nature; both these natures produce fruit (or evidence). Right in the middle of this discourse (verse 18), Paul clears up our thinking "But if you are led by the Spirit, you are not under law".

There is another way to live that is superior to the natural system of principles and methods of behavior. This old system is no better that superstition; it depends on the fulfillment of a human action for God's favor to be present. Take tithing as an example; we are exhorted to tithe as a way of expressing our gratefulness to God, but it is always tied to the release of God's blessing.

Jesus abolished the old way in favor of a love with no strings attached, "I will bless just because it is what I do, and all you need to do is rest in my love for you".

This is the way of the Spirit - dare we believe that God's love could be so good.

If we can only catch a glimpse of the scale of his love, then we will surrender our entire existence into his care. All attempts to satisfy a God who is already completely satisfied will end, we will let go of the compulsion to 'live right' as the means for attracting God's blessing, and rest in the outrageous notion

Chapter 18. Life-Principles V. Surrender.

that 'blessing us' is God's idea not ours, and all we have to do is stop trying so hard, and let him.

This is scary stuff so I feel compelled to make a short clarification:

I am not advocating irresponsible or selfish behavior, but I am saying that if we think that our behavior in any way curries favor with God, then we make a mockery of the costly price Christ paid for our freedom from works of the flesh.

Our natural minds attempt to repel such thinking in the same way that our body attempts to repel a virus, our natural minds have reduced the work of Christ to a scale that is palatable to the flesh – and as a result Christianity has become 'all about us'.

We must re-elevate Christ to the surpassing greatness, and the unsearchable wonder, that Paul described – to do less is to settle for a form of Christianity that barely requires the Spirit at all… *(Trust me, I've been there).*

When our security with God is based on the observable lifestyle we adopt, the Spirit of God is relegated to the side lines – much like an emergency player on a football team that is only called upon if the need arises.

If we harbor the lie 'the flesh counts', then in reality our surrender is toward the flesh, and not the Spirit. These two are not companions, they are bitter enemies, we cannot allocate our allegiance to them according to the circumstances we face – the Spirit gives life, he requires our total abandon to his goodness for this life to flow to us.

Chapter 19.
The Spirit Gives Life.

At a glance the first part of John 6:63 "The Spirit gives life" seems to be a somewhat benign statement. It may well be true, but it seems to be more of a general statement, than one with very specific intent. So we read over it, and continue our search for the key to unlock God's involvement in our lives.

In so doing we have just passed over the very thing we search for.

The 'life' that Jesus describes in John 10:10 "I came to give you Life" is what we were born for. God's master plan was for us to possess the same life as him – and Jesus came to return it to us.

We can easily become confused by the many references to 'life' in the bible; spiritual life, eternal life, everlasting life, the river of life, the tree of life – these are all pointing to Mr. Life himself (Jesus). If we have one, then we have all – because these are all contained in Jesus, and we have him without limit.

For instance; when we are born-again our spirit is given spiritual life, at that same moment in time we also become eternal beings (eternal life), our existence as citizens of planet earth ends and we become citizens of heaven (everlasting life), we feed on Christ (the Tree of life), and we are participants in the blessings of heaven (the River of life). These all happen simultaneously, they are one life-giving event, and they are all present tense and ours by simply believing in Jesus.

There is no believer who's spirit has been made alive, that does not also possess eternal life – they are exactly the same event. There is no maturing process required for us to progress from one to the other; they all become ours in the twinkling of an eye when we are saved.

It is also quite possible to possess this life in all its fullness, and not actually live as if it is there. Christ has wrought an amazing work in our lives, whether we see it, and live from the truth of it, is up to us.

To live from the truth of it is not simply a matter of busily going about the activities of Christianity; rather, it is to see the transformative work that Christ completed in us when he gave us life, and resting in the ability of that divine life to produce fruit.

This is hard for many because we are pre-programmed by the old Adamic nature to seek-out the human factor. It would not be such a problem if the intention of God was to purpose us for a life of good works, but that was not his intention – he put to death our Old Nature, so that Christ himself could be re-born in us as the power house of our lives.

It is our habitual promotion of the flesh that obstructs and obscures the unsearchable greatness of Christ. The result is that the Christian life is more defined by good works (with a courteous nod to Christ), that by the magnificent splendor of the Prince of Heaven himself.

> *We know Christ is there somewhere;*
> *we are just too distracted to discover him.*

When we take a step back from our compulsive ways and 'be still', we can begin the adventure we were made for; 'Christ in me'.

As I said this is hard for many, it seems so reckless and irresponsible at first, yet slowly as we learn to fix our eyes on him we begin to experience a new dawning. Over time we learn to hush the insistent echo of the flesh.

CHAPTER 19. THE SPIRIT GIVES LIFE.

It is a slow process, much like a rose bud opening to the warm rays of the sun. One petal at a time the rose uncovers its inner beauty as the unrelenting warm radiance breaks through. Our insecurities are like those rose petals, the more the radiant life of Christ is allowed in, the more our reluctance disappears and we expose our true self – *the perfect image of Christ appears.* We were not created to be balled-up tight like a bud, we were created to respond to Christ's radiant love – and just like the bud, we cannot force ourselves to bloom, we can only do it in response to the loving glow of Christ.

We must discover this glow, each one of us.

As Jesus said in Matthew 11:29 "we must learn of him" - *if we are to find rest for our souls.* Even if it takes a month, even a year – we must learn of him. If we do nothing else, it matters not – <u>we must learn of him</u>.

> *We must discover a love so strong, that we stop fighting it…*
> *and let ourselves be loved.*

We don't easily let ourselves be loved, it goes against all we have been taught to be so self-indulgent – yet it is why Jesus came, he came to give us himself. He came to break through our self-made hearts of stone and let him love us. Love us for his reasons. Not because of our self-constructed value, but because he is love, and he died so that his love could make its home in our hearts.

If we have any purpose while we walk upon this earth it is this; we must discover his love.

> *Every other human pursuit is vain, but for this one glorious quest*
> *– to discover the unspeakable love of Christ,*
> *and surrender every fiber of our being into its stunning glory.*

The Lie We Like Best

Our pilgrimage upon this earth is not a progression through various struggles and experiences designed to bring us to maturity in God (sorry Mr. Bunyan) - we have no quest but to discover Christ, it is our sole obsession and pursuit, just to know him. Our earthly experiences are not the workshop God uses to shape us, it is the cross of Christ that does that – our only part is to grasp the scale and wonder of it, and lean-in to its transformative power.

We are not transformed by the stuff of this earthly walk (that was Adam's approach) – we are transformed by the heart of Christ. If we allow the hard knocks of planet earth to be our making, then the work of Christ is relegated to mere speculation and superstition.

But Christ did (in the blink of an eye), that which the natural world couldn't complete in a lifetime – he made us fit to be with God, *and we had no say in the matter.*

For this reason it is imperative that we gain a clear view of the love of Christ and all that it means. A view that is interpreted through his unrelenting, radiant heart of love - not our conditional, performance-based hearts.

This view is only found at the foot of the cross.

The foot of the cross has become something of a cliché in Christian circles, yet few actually know how to linger there. We know how to spend time in church, or watching the God channel on TV, but we are less at home gazing at the cross of Christ. I am not talking of our times of daily prayer or meditation, but a deep inner quest to understand and absorb the love of Jesus that surpasses knowledge.

Paul expressed it so well in Ephesians 3:18-9 "…that we may have power, together with all the saints, to comprehend the length and width and height and depth of His love, and to know the love of Christ that surpasses knowledge, that you may be filled with all the fullness of God."

A deep revelation of the love of Christ is the pre-cursor to being 'filled with all the fullness of God'.

Chapter 19. The Spirit Gives Life.

The love of Christ surpasses human knowledge, yet we have contained it so neatly within our clichés and praise songs – it can't be contained, and it can't be known… *but for the individual pilgrimage each of us must make to the foot of the cross.*

Without such a pilgrimage we are limited to the generalizations of the culture of Christianity, but with it we step into a form of Christianity that was previously unknown to us – it is a Christianity that is carried aloft upon the heart of Christ, it is what we were made for.

Chapter 20.
The Foot Of The Cross.

WHAT lies at the foot of the cross?

If we could locate the exact spot where the crucifixion took place on that hill outside Jerusalem, we might find some dry rubble, perhaps a religious relic, or a well-worn trail – but it is not a pilgrimage to this natural environment that we need to make. Our pilgrimage is to a far more profound location than the earthly site of Christ's death, our pilgrimage is to the place where he lives today, it is a journey of the heart to observe and discover the invisible outcomes of his death and resurrection.

The location of Christ's physical death may hold a fascination for some of us, just as the other iconic places of his life may intrigue us. But the new life we have in Christ takes us beyond the ritual of visiting places of religious importance - why would we visit the places where Christ lived and died 2000 years ago, *when we can visit his present day home, and meet with him in real time.*

Christianity is not a pilgrimage through past events and places; it is a present tense revelation of the eternal outcomes of those past events, and a personal identification with them to the point where we too live as truly eternal people.

This kind of transformation does not take place simply by visiting a location where a historically significant event occurred. It takes place when we visit Christ himself, and we determine that his life and death has put an end to human history as we knew it – we have become those for whom eternity is their present day existence.

These words roll off the tongue easily, but their real import is not as easily gained.

To a large extent this is because the culture of Christianity holds us in the natural realm through its many activities and causes, so our real identity teeters between two worlds.

So how do we escape the gravitational pull of the natural realm, and make our own unique and individual pilgrimage to Christ? How does one actually visit Christ?

In the end it all comes down to the improbable notion that there is more to Christianity than we are presently experiencing. If we can cross over that line, then a future awaits us that makes the old pale by comparison - but we must leave the past and all of its religious mindsets behind us, to enter into it.

This new vista of Christ is quite unlike the old. The old view was based on a lie *(you know the one)*.

With the lie out of the way, Christ is seen in an entirely different way. Whereas in the past he was perceived primarily through the lens of 'the purposes of the flesh', he is now perceived through the lens of the 'purposes of the Spirit'.

The 'purposes of the flesh' are all about the validation of humanity through its own self-generated activities and lifestyle. These activities might include church involvement, good deeds, charity, ministries, and the various causes of the needy. While these all have merit, they do not actually validate us - for that we need to discover the purposes of the Spirit.

The Spirit has one over-arching purpose - 'that we be found in Christ'.

Chapter 20. The Foot Of The Cross.

At first glance this doesn't sound like enough, but when we discover the astounding scale of this statement, it is truly mind-blowing *(or to use Paul's words, it is vast, immeasurable, and unsearchable).*

The first surprise we get as we begin to view the cross of Christ is that the flow is one-directional. We are used to a form of Christianity which is directed by us toward God; we worship, we serve, we give – all with God as the objective of these activities. It comes as quite a surprise to find God is outward focused not inward, he is not attempting to draw anything out of us - but instead wishes to fill us with his life.

It takes quite some adjusting to accept that God gives to us, quite apart from our performance as his kids. I always thought God was measuring my output, and that life was a journey of 'giving to God' – but I know now that it is the other way around, God doesn't want my best – he wants to give me his best.

He wants me to stop trying to 'do' for him, and begin to 'rest in' what he has done for me. Acts 17:24-25 says, "The God who made the world and everything in it … is not served by human hands, *as if he needed anything*".

What a clarifying scripture. If God is not served by human hands – then we must find a new context for scriptures like Romans 12:1 "offer your bodies as living sacrifices, holy and pleasing to God – this is your spiritual act of worship".

The only possible conclusion is that God wants us to surrender ourselves to his desire to fill us with his life. Any other human response is incapable of presenting a spiritual act of worship that is holy and pleasing to him. Only his own holiness is good enough to please him, and he gives it to us, so that we too can please him.

He doesn't want my best lifestyle or good deeds as the catalyst to release his favor and blessing, he wants me to empty myself of the security that is found in 'what I do', and rest in the scandalous notion that Christ has done enough. My only part is to give myself over to this radical gospel and entrust myself fully into the goodness of God, then I become a living sacrifice – *as I rest in his sacrifice.*

This is the astounding message of the gospel that I had been missing. Christ entered the human arena and made a way for his life to flow through the hearts of men once again. I have two options: 1. I can construct a response based on my own best endeavors, 2. I can lose myself into Christ's best endeavors.

Option 1. Is a feeble sacrifice constructed from humanity's weakness, it keeps alive the very problem that caused all the trouble in the beginning – man cannot create spiritual life.

Option 2. I become hidden in Christ's sacrifice; I am translated into Christ's work on the cross by faith. As I lift my eyes off my own best efforts and rest in his, I actually become the sacrifice of Christ – his spiritual life flows through me.

> **As I mentioned earlier, this spiritual life is one-directional.**
> **Christ gives – I receive.**

The flesh does not take this lying down; it does not relish the idea that it cannot give life. It is here that the battle ground for the mind of the Christian takes place.

The second surprise as we scan the vast horizons of the 'cross of Christ' is the absence of any human contribution. It is the loneliest place in history, his Father appears to have withdrawn, and we are counted amongst the mockers. Christ is a solitary figure who bears the fallen nature of humanity alone, every sinful heart *(since Adam - until the end of time),* is concentrated into his spirit. No one lifts a finger to help, not one person in the whole of human history can share his load – he is slain in solitude.

He dies the spiritual death of humanity, *all by himself.*

Chapter 20. The Foot Of The Cross.

The solitary nature of Christ's death is important, because it sets the pattern for all that follows.

<u>We do not contribute to his death - and we do not contribute to his life.</u>

Christ stands alone as the sole provider of everything that humanity needs. He died our death, and he lives our life. We have been side-lined from the task of contributing in any way to the spiritual environment of our life - *Christ has taken over our spirit.*

Before we knew Christ, our spirit was a container for the spiritual death which was in satan - now it is the container for the spiritual life which is in Christ. Christ has taken possession of us, and he has freed us from the death-grip of satan.

Each individual receives this new life separately. We receive it by viewing the work of Christ on the cross, and choosing to make it the defining truth of our life. It does not become ours by joining a church or even repeating the sinners prayer, it becomes our when we let go of our self-made life, and caste ourselves in to Christ's life.

Christ endured death as a solitary man, and we partake of him as solitary men and women. This is repentance, we individually ask Christ to possess our spirit. We thank Jesus for giving us the chance to become a son/daughter of God, and ask him to fill us up with himself – this he does instantly, and we are re-born of God.

The importance of this one-on-one exchange cannot be overstated; we cannot be overtaken and possessed by the Spirit of Christ without it. Christ does not push his way in, or provide access to his divine life by virtue of our involvement in a church or denomination, he says "come to me" – and each of us must come to him, *all by ourselves.*

Christ's life is one-directional, it flows to us by faith only, *(independently of our best spiritual activities),* we must each individually view the claims of the cross of Christ, and choose them as our own – and then the greatest surprise of all is revealed, we become joined to Christ – he died our death, and now he lives our life.

Chapter 21.
He Lives My Life.

I know…..
the things I am writing about are pretty close to the edge for many people, the idea that Christ lives my life for me, is way out there – but let's unpack it… *(before you declare me crazy).*

We know that in Galatians 2:20 Paul declares "I no longer live, but Christ lives in me". We also know that in John 17:26 Jesus says "I have made you known to them, and will continue to make you known in order that the love you have for me may be in them and that I myself may be in them".

Question: What is Jesus doing in us? Is anything going on - or is he just kind of *hovering* there?

Keeping us company perhaps, guiding us home, maybe just keeping an eye on us… he must be doing something - he doesn't take possession of people for no reason. Surely he hasn't made his home in us to just observe our lives - there has to be a more profound reason why the Prince of Glory would take residence within mere men.

In the book of John, Jesus compares 'his presence within us' to 'the Fathers presence within him'. John 14:20 "On that day you will know that I am in my Father, and you are in me, and I am in you".

He also describes in the book of John how this 'presence within him' plays out in his life - John 14:10 "…it is the Father, living in me, who is doing his work" and in John 5:19 "…the Son can do nothing by himself". The comparison to us, is found in John 3:21 "But whoever lives by the truth comes into the light, so that it may be plainly seen that what he has done has been done through God".

It was the Father *living in Jesus* who did the work - and for us, it is when we come into the light *(are in union with Jesus)* that the work we do, is done through God. Some translations say that the works are done 'in God' and some say 'by God' – the important thing is that God is the life-force that produces the work.

Not that we are robots, manipulated by Jesus as he works the controls *(with no will of our own)* – rather, we are hidden in his divine nature, and as this nature becomes clearer and clearer to us, we begin to place our confidence in his work on the cross, and his Spirit is expressed through us. This confidence causes us to rely on him for the expression of his Spirit, instead of our own self-generated works.

This is how Jesus operated. When Jesus said he only does what he saw his Father doing, he didn't mean that he saw his Father doing a miracle in heaven and he copied him on earth - but rather, the life source that was in his Father also flowed through him as he surrendered himself to his Father's love and goodness.

The difference between works generated by our compulsion to 'do good things' to please God, and works generated by the indwelling presence of God's goodness in us, is paramount. The first is the expression of 'the flesh counts', the second is the expression of 'the Spirit gives life'.

This is the mystery that Paul spoke about in Colossians and Ephesians. Colossians 1:27 "To them God has chosen to make known among the Gentiles the glorious riches of this mystery, which is Christ in you, the hope of glory".

Chapter 21. He Lives My Life.

At first glance this seems to be suggesting that Christ is a deposit that is made in to our lives, that keeps our hope focused on our eternal glory. But we know from John 5:24 that we have already crossed over from death to life – we know that eternal life began in the instant we were born again, *we are already in glory*. In John 17:22-23 Jesus prays these words "I have given them the glory that you gave me, that they may be one as we are one. I in them, and you in me".

If we can unlock the mystery of 'Christ in me' then the 'hope of glory' – becomes today's 'reality of glory'.

But what is this glory?

It is the display of God's divine attributes and perfection – and in relation to us, it is the manifestation of God's perfect nature living itself out through us. It is interesting that when Moses asked God to 'show him his glory' in Exodus 33:18, God replied "I myself will make all my 'goodness' pass before you…" Moses asked God to let him see his <u>glory</u> - so God showed him his <u>goodness</u>. God's perfect and good nature is his glory – *and Jesus says that he has given it to us.*

God has expressed his glory in physical terms also, through bright light, fire, clouds, and in many other visible ways. God's manifest glory is the visible expression of his extraordinary goodness. His glory is not the visible radiance, it is his invisible divine goodness – and this goodness is so magnificent that it has a radiance that outshines the universe.

In the Old Testament this glory was expressed from time to time as God manifested himself into the lives of men and women. Now God's glory has been permanently manifest in us, we are the container of the glory of God in the physical realm – our spirits are filled with Jesus, and our bodies are walking-around the manifest glory of God 24/7. This is more than the stunning and intricate creation of the human form; it is the divine God himself who outshines the universe, and has made his home in us.

Christ in you, the hope of glory.

The angels see this glory in us, even the demons and satan himself see this glory – it shines in the realm of the spirit as we rest in the accomplishments of Christ. The important thing is that we also see it, and lose ourselves into its astounding truth.

The mystery has been revealed… *but few want it.*

Why? Because we love the lie. 1 Corinthians 1:29-31 says that God chose the lowly and despised things of the world… "that no flesh should <u>glory</u> in His presence". The flesh wants to glory in its achievements; Adam started the ball rolling, and it is still going strong. But the glory of Christ *(which is in us)*, cannot be manifest alongside the vain-glory of the flesh. So instead our lives shine forth the very weak light of the flesh, when we have the potential for the astounding, radiant glory of Christ.

> *That is why the mystery of 'Christ in us' remains but a hope…*
> *it awaits the embrace of the spirits of men.*

This mystery will not force anyone to yield control. Yet if we could only see the magnificence of his glory, and imagine a life surrendered to his goodness *(and by comparison the dim glow of the works of the flesh)* – then we would let go of all our striving in a heartbeat, and lean-in to his desire to live his life in and through us.

CONCLUSION.

This book is the second book in a series of three.

In the first book in the series 'Back in the Garden again', I presented a different view of things. A view that has at its core the notion that Christ came to restore humanity to its original form - *the way it was in Eden before there was sin.* This original form becomes ours again as we take the step from death to life, by receiving Christ.

This book is a progression of the first. It examines the superior value that fallen humanity has assigned to the flesh – and then it presents the case; 'The Spirit gives life and the flesh counts for nothing'. For us to enter into this life a major shift in thinking must occur – we must acknowledge the lie, and relegate it to the scrap heap where it belongs.

The third and final book in the series contemplates a future without the lie in operation. It casts its gaze over the most spectacular landscape ever presented to humanity; 'the glory of Christ in me'. It is a mystery that has been hidden for ages by the demanding nature of the flesh - as we peel back the veil cast by this old thinking, we begin to glimpse the unsearchable riches of Christ.

We cannot overstate the extravagance of the salvation that Jesus purchased for us. The horizon of the wonders of his goodness and love always stretches further before us, calling us to let go, and come further and deeper into him.

Deeper than was ever possible through the means of 'lifestyle-based' Christianity, and can only be found by personally discovering the love that Jesus expressed on the cross.

It is a salvation that scandalizes the limitations that religion has placed on to Christ, and it is a salvation that dares us to believe that God could be bigger and better and stronger that we ever before imagined… *and it awaits us all.*

This salvation does not require our engagement through religion or lifestyle, it is already engaged into us by the indwelling Christ – all that remains is that we see the scale of the union with God that we are in, and abandon ourselves to the adventure of it.

> *We were originally designed, and then re-born, for this union -*
> *it is our true destiny and glorious obsession,*
> *and it lays waiting inside every believer, anticipating our surrender to it,*
> *so that together with Jesus we might soar upon the breath of God's love.*

Some will find this salvation so unlike the one that they have known; that it will barely seem that we are discussing the same events - *the life, death and resurrection of Jesus.* The lie has trapped us inside a salvation that is meager compared to the true reality which is ours in Christ. It is like being trapped inside the tomb of Christ, instead of bursting free with him into his eternal glory.

Join me for one more conversation… *the surpassing greatness of Christ.*

www.ingramcontent.com/pod-product-compliance
Lightning Source LLC
Chambersburg PA
CBHW070627300426
44113CB00010B/1685